Ancient Anatolia

A Captivating Guide to Ancient Civilizations of Asia Minor, Including the Hittite Empire, Arameans, Luwians, Neo-Assyrian Empire, Cimmerians, Scythians, Persians, Romans, and More

© **Copyright 2019**

All Rights Reserved. No part of this book may be reproduced in any form without permission in writing from the author. Reviewers may quote brief passages in reviews.

Disclaimer: No part of this publication may be reproduced or transmitted in any form or by any means, mechanical or electronic, including photocopying or recording, or by any information storage and retrieval system, or transmitted by email without permission in writing from the publisher.

While all attempts have been made to verify the information provided in this publication, neither the author nor the publisher assumes any responsibility for errors, omissions or contrary interpretations of the subject matter herein.

This book is for entertainment purposes only. The views expressed are those of the author alone, and should not be taken as expert instruction or commands. The reader is responsible for his or her own actions.

Adherence to all applicable laws and regulations, including international, federal, state and local laws governing professional licensing, business practices, advertising and all other aspects of doing business in the US, Canada, UK or any other jurisdiction is the sole responsibility of the purchaser or reader.

Neither the author nor the publisher assumes any responsibility or liability whatsoever on the behalf of the purchaser or reader of these materials. Any perceived slight of any individual or organization is purely unintentional.

Free Bonus from Captivating History (Available for a Limited time)

Hi History Lovers!

Now you have a chance to join our exclusive history list so you can get your first history ebook for free as well as discounts and a potential to get more history books for free! Simply visit the link below to join.

Captivatinghistory.com/ebook

Also, make sure to follow us on Facebook, Twitter and Youtube by searching for Captivating History.

Contents

INTRODUCTION 1

CHAPTER 1 – THE HITTITE EMPIRE 3

CHAPTER 2 – THE ARAMEAN CONFEDERATION 14

CHAPTER 3 – THE LUWIANS 18

CHAPTER 4 – THE NEO-ASSYRIAN EMPIRE 37

CHAPTER 5 – THE CIMMERIANS 61

CHAPTER 6 – THE SCYTHIANS 67

CHAPTER 7 – THE PERSIANS 77

CHAPTER 8 – THE SELEUCID EMPIRE AND ROMANS IN ANATOLIA 97

CONCLUSION 104

REFERENCES 108

Introduction

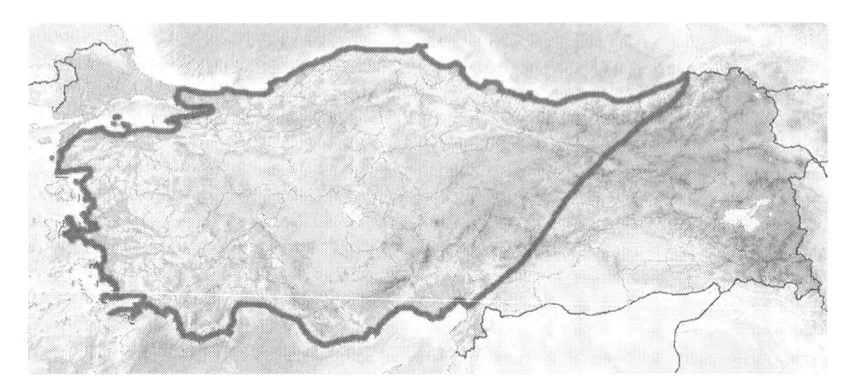

Map of Anatolia

What sparks curiosity about ancient Anatolia, which makes up most of modern-day Turkey, in the minds of history lovers is the diversity of its peoples throughout its territories and time. This book seeks to present the most current view on the events that unfolded through the centuries of the Bronze and Iron Ages of Anatolia. The reader can follow the rise of some of the most famous empires in the world, as well as learn about the circumstances that led to their fall. From early settlements of nomadic tribes to the creation of vast empires, Anatolia changed its face numerous times throughout history. Not just territories and kingdoms changed, but the people inhabiting it also did so as well, in their language, culture, and religion.

Even though they were faced with a lack of evidence for certain periods of ancient Anatolia, or for certain peoples, historians seek to accurately paint the picture of the lives in all the various kingdoms of Anatolia. This book follows the Hittite Empire in its rise and fall. It discusses the Arameans and the influence of their culture on the civilized world, as well as the influence of the Luwians and their dispersion throughout Anatolia. Even if they were never able to organize a united Luwian Empire, they changed all the kingdoms they came in contact with. The effects of this ancient civilization can still be felt today as certain dialects of the Luwian language still exist in Anatolia.

Furthermore, this book follows the rise of one of the largest empires of the Iron Age, the Neo-Assyrian Empire. The reader will get to know the accomplishments of the Assyrian kings and generals and the decisions they made that led to its fall. The vacuum of power that was left after the fall of the Assyrian Empire was filled with the deeds of the Cimmerians and the Scythians, nomadic peoples who fought for their right to exist in Anatolia.

The story doesn't end with them, however. Another great empire of the Iron Age, the Persian Empire, also expanded its territories through Anatolia. This book will discuss the Achaemenid dynasty and introduce the reader to Xerxes the Great, who fought at the famous Battle of Thermopylae where 300 Spartans, among others, lost their lives defending all of Greece.

The end of the book is reserved for the Romans and their own influence on the Anatolian kingdoms, as their politics gradually led to the creation of new territories, territories which had once been known as great empires but were now reduced to being provinces of Rome.

Ancient Anatolia was as diverse in its landscape as in the cultures that inhabited it, from the mountainous regions perfect for nomadic tribes and their herds to the rich valleys of rivers that were the fertile grounds for the births of great civilizations. Anatolia is rich in archeological findings, and the human effort to lift the veil of mystery that encompasses it is still ongoing.

Chapter 1 – The Hittite Empire

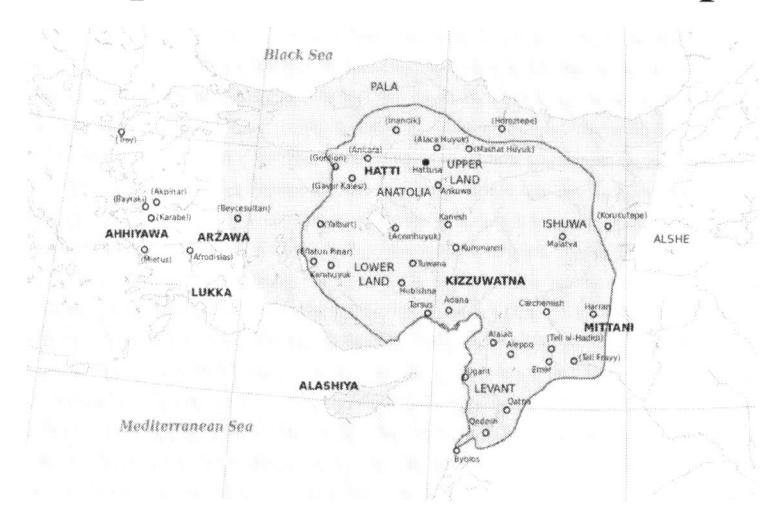

Map of Hittite Empire at its greatest extent, circa 1350 to 1300 BCE, represented by the green line

The name "Hittite" refers to the people who were the inhabitants of north-central Anatolia. This land was called Hatti, and it was referred to even in the Bible. It is still unknown where the origin of the Hittite people lies, but it is known that they came to Anatolia before 2000 BCE. It is speculated that they came from the lands around the Sea of Azov in today's Ukraine because of the Indo-European language similarities.

The arrival of the Hittites in Anatolia was intrusive for the native culture there, as the Hittites brought Indo-European elements along with them. It is unknown if the means of this intrusiveness were due to conquest or the gradual assimilation of the natives into the new culture of the recently arrived Hittites.

For several centuries after their arrival, there were some difficulties in establishing a single nation. Separate groups of Hittites were centered around some major cities, and strong leadership was needed to bring these groups together in order to conquer a large part of central Anatolia and establish a kingdom with its capital, which would be known as Hattusa.

The empire was founded by King Labarna I, probably in early 1600 BCE. The only original sources we have from this period come from copies of tablets from the 17th century BCE. The copies are Akkadian in origin and were made in the 14th and 13th centuries BCE; therefore, some of the information remains unclear. It is unknown whether the founder of the Hittite Empire was actually Labarna I or Hattusili I, who also had Labarna in his name, as it was used as a title. Some historians think these two figures are actually the same person, but Hittite chronologies treat Labarna I as the predecessor of Hattusili I, who would then be known as Labarna II.

Labarna I is considered the traditional founder of the Hittite Old Kingdom, and his wife was known only by her title Tawannanna. This title was passed down to a new queen upon the death of the current queen. Even a successor's wife wouldn't obtain the title as long as the old queen lived. This means that if Tawannanna died before the king, the title would have been passed either to her daughter or to the new wife of the king. Tawannanna had the duty of ruling the kingdom while the king was absent, usually fighting in battles. She was also a high priestess of the empire, and the king was considered to be the high priest. Very little is known about King

Labarna I, other than the fact that he established rule over the Hittite empire until the early years of the Iron Age.

However, Hattusili I is remembered for his military campaigns that expanded the kingdom. He conquered the areas south and north of Hattusa, and he also took his armies west, into the Arzawan lands (western Anatolia), and southeast into the Syrian kingdom of Yamhad. But only his successor and grandson, Mursili I, managed to successfully finish the campaign in Syria. In 1595, Mursili I sacked Aleppo, which was at that time the capital of the kingdom of Yamhad. During the same year, he took his army down the Euphrates River and captured Mari (located in modern-day Syria) and Babylonia. He also ransacked the city of Babylon in 1531 BCE. Instead of joining Babylonia to the Hittite Empire, Mursili I chose to give control over it to his Kassite allies, who would rule it for over 500 years. However, internal disagreements in the Hittite state made Mursili retreat with his army. The remaining years of the 16th century BCE were filled with dynastic quarrels and the war with their eastern neighbors, the Hurrians. Mursili was assassinated shortly after his retreat from his conquests, and this event marked a period of chaos in the Hittite Empire. The Hurrians, people who lived along the upper Tigris and Euphrates Rivers, took the opportunity and conquered Aleppo and the surrounding areas. They also conquered the coastal part of Adanuya, which they renamed to Kizzuwatna.

There is very little evidence of what happened following these events inside the Hittite Empire itself. It is considered that after strong leadership came a series of weak ones, and this pattern of conquering and losing lands repeated itself multiple times during the next 500 years of the Old Kingdom. The structure of Hittite kingship may be the reason for this pattern to occur so often. The king wasn't regarded as a living god by his subjects but rather as the first amongst equals. However, between 1400 BCE and 1200 BCE, the kings became stronger and centralized their power.

The next prominent king of the Old Kingdom was Telipinu, who reigned from circa 1525 until 1500 BCE. Soon after taking the throne, his son and wife were killed by his rivals. At first, the assassins were sentenced to death; however, the new king wanted to put a stop to the internal feuds, and so, he decided to banish the assassins and his rivals rather than sentence them to death. In the following years, Telipinu made an alliance with the Hurrians from Kizzuwatna, and with their help, he took back some of the former Hittite lands. This king is mostly known for drawing up the edict of Telipinu, which set up laws of succession for the throne. Up to this point, the laws were vague, and the Hittite Empire had constant conflicts between the southern and eastern branches of the royal family. The edict was clear that the firstborn son should always be the successor. In case of his untimely death, the second-born son would succeed the throne. If a king had no sons, a daughter's husband would become king. However, after Telipinu's death, the Hittite Empire entered what is known as the "dark age," which would last for approximately seventy years. Historians do not know why exactly this occurred as they do not have any sources from which to draw any major conclusions.

With the death of Telipinu in 1500, the Old Kingdom ceased to exist, and a period known as the Middle Kingdom started. In this period, the Hittites were under constant attack, mainly by the Kaskas, who settled along the coast of the Black Sea. During this period, the Hittites had to move their capital, first to Sapinuwa and then to Samuha. During the Middle Kingdom, the Hittites developed skills of international politics and diplomacy. They were the first known people who practiced making alliances and conducting treaties. During this period, the Hittite religion went through some changes, and they adopted several new gods and rituals from their Hurrian neighbors.

With King Tudhaliya I in the early 14th century BCE, the Hittites entered another period known as the New Kingdom. During this time, another set of changes in the kingdom were made, and kings became more powerful by establishing themselves as being more than human. People started referring to them as "my Sun." This is also the period when kings took the role of high priests, and they started conducting festivals and their yearly tours of holy places. Tudhaliya I expanded the kingdom to the west, encroaching on the territory of Arzawa. He also defeated the Hurrians in their states of Aleppo and Mitanni. But after his death, one more last weak period came when the Hittites lost most of their lands, with even Hattusa being raided.

However, with King Suppiluliuma I, the Hittite Empire recovered its former glory. He was the son of Tudhaliya II and Queen Daduhepa, and he ruled between 1344 and 1322 BCE. Suppiluliuma was famous for being a proficient warrior and statesmen, and he is known for challenging the Egyptian Empire that was dominating Asia Minor at the time. Suppiluliuma I bound himself to the neighboring states by marrying his sister to the king of Hayasan and his daughter to the king of the Arzawan state of Mira. He himself married a Babylonian princess named Malignal and gained control over Arzawan territory. One of the source texts mentions Suppiluliuma's first wife, Queen Henti, who was banished by her husband so he could marry the Babylonian princess for the state's advantage. This Queen Henti is considered to be the mother of all the sons King Suppiluliuma I had. He was victorious in the war against the Hurrian kingdom of Mitanni, which he made a client state and gave to his own son-in-law, Shattiwazza.

At that time, in Egypt, Pharaoh Akhenaten led a turmoil government. Suppiluliuma I seized the opportunity and took control over Amurru, an Egyptian territory in Syria. This was actually not achieved by war but by the decision of Amurru's ruler to join the Hittites instead of shedding blood on the battlefield. This event was enough to destabilize the vassal kingdoms of Egypt and to incite revolts. Suppiluliuma I was so strong that even the Egyptian queen of Tutankhamen, who had recently died, sent him a letter, asking him to send one of his sons to Egypt to marry her and rule as king. She did this to avoid being married to a mere "servant of the kingdom," which was thought to either be the Egyptian general Horemheb or Tutankhamun's vizier Ay. Suppiluliuma sent ambassadors to investigate the truthfulness of the letter, and upon their confirmation, he sent his son Zannanza to Egypt, who unfortunately died on his way there. This marriage alliance with Egypt never came to pass, and Suppiluliuma exchanged angry letters with the new pharaoh of Egypt, Ay, who Suppiluliuma blamed for the death of Zannanza. Soon after, Suppiluliuma I died of the plague, which is believed to have been introduced in the Hittite Empire by Egyptian slaves.

Suppiluliuma I was succeeded by his eldest son, Arnuwanda II, in 1322, who, like his father, soon died of the plague. After him, the throne was occupied by Mursili II, his younger brother, who ruled between 1321 and 1295 BCE. Early in his reign, he faced various rebellions from his own people, as well as contempt from his enemies. The most serious rebellions were in the mountain regions of Anatolia, initiated by the Kaskas, and in the southwest of Asia Minor, in the Arzawa kingdom. The general opinion was that Mursili II was an inexperienced ruler who only became king because of his brother's death. Even though he was young, he was certainly not a child. He had two older brothers who would have inherited the throne if Mursili wasn't of the right age to rule on his own. His brothers were serving as viceroys of Carchemish and Aleppo.

When it came to military campaigns and diplomacy, Mursili proved himself to be more than competent. He secured the northern borders of his kingdom by defeating the Kaskas in just the first two years of his reign. Immediately after, he had to fight Unhaziti, the king of Arzawa, in the west, as he tried to separate the Hittites from their allies. Mursili also attacked a city called Millawanda, which would later be known as Miletus. The annals surviving from Mursili's time are revealing as they show there was a solar eclipse in the tenth year of his reign, and it was regarded as an omen, as he was preparing to attack the Kaskas one more time.

After Mursili II, the throne went to his eldest son, Muwatalli II, who ruled from around 1295 to 1272 BCE). Not long after he came to power, Muwatalli II decided to move the capital from Hattusa to a city he named Tarhuntassa. He appointed his brother, Hattusili, as the governor of Hattusa. The reason for this change is unknown, but based on texts written in the time of Hattusili III's reign, there could be two possibilities.

The first is that Muwatalli decided to move the capital because Hattusa was near the northern border, which was under constant military threat due to Kaskian skirmishes. This move to the southern territory of the kingdom could mean safety from the turbulent northern border, but it would also be a good stratetical position for the fight against Egypt over Syria, which was about to start.

The second theory as to why Muwatalli moved the capital involves religious reasons. He implemented some changes to the state religion; more specifically, he worshiped a new storm god, whose cult's seat of power was farther to the west. He introduced this god of storms, named Umarmungsszene, in his new royal seals, and all the kings that came after him used the same motif on their seals.

Muwatalli II is best known as the Hittite king who battled against Ramesses II in the Battle of Kadesh around 1274 BCE. Kadesh was a city on the Orontes River, near today's Lebanon-Syria border. This battle is important as it is the earliest recorded battle, which included details of tactics and army formations. It was probably the largest chariot battle ever fought; the estimation is that there were 5,000 to 6,000 chariots fighting in the battle.

At the time of this battle, the Hittite's economy was largely dependent on the control of trade routes. Northern Syria was one of the most important routes for trade, as well as a source of metal for the entire empire, and this is why it needed to be protected against any possible attacks. The defense of this important Hittite area was put to the test by Ramesses II, as he wanted to expand Egypt's territories. In the spring of 1274, Ramesses II launched a military campaign with the intention of restoring territories Egypt had possessed almost a century before. To stop Ramesses, Muwatalli marched with his army to the south to confront him.

The Egyptian army consisted of four divisions: Amun, Re, Seth, and a newly created division called Ptah. There are mentions of one more troop named Nrrn or Ne'arin, which were most likely mercenaries loyal to Egypt, but they were left behind in Amurru to defend the port of Sumur. They would later play a critical role in the Battle of Kadesh. Another group of mercenaries in the Egyptian army was the Sherden troops, who were a group of Sea Peoples, possibly Akkadian. It is worth mentioning that the Sherden people's first mention in history was found in a text from the records of Ramesses II, who fought them in defense of Egypt's Mediterranean coast and later incorporated them in his personal guard.

On Muwatalli's side, the Hittites gathered all of their allies, with King Rimisharrinaa of Aleppo among them. Records of Ramesses II mention nineteen allies who helped the Hittites in the great Battle of Kadesh. The extent of Hittite influence is observed here, as such a large number of allied states came to help them.

The tactics Muwatalli used in this battle are very interesting since it is the first time historical records show the use of deception as a military tactic. Muwatalli ordered two of his spies to act as deserters and run to the Egyptian side. Once they gained Ramesses' ear, they told him Muwatalli and his army were still at Aleppo, far away. Muwatalli was actually camped at Kadesh, waiting for Ramesses in ambush. Soon after, Ramesses learned about Muwatalli's trickery and managed to defeat the division that attacked his camp. However, the rest of Ramesses' army was still farther south, fighting Muwatalli's second division. The following day, the Egyptians won the battle.

Ramesses II gave special attention to this battle and created two versions of it. One is considered poetic, as he depicts himself as a powerful military leader who made Muwatalli shrink in fear. But the other one, in the form of bulleting, tells a story of the struggles the Egyptian army went through during the battle. Muwatalli was forced to retreat inside Kadesh's fort, but the Egyptians didn't have enough resources to maintain a siege. The battle ended up badly for both sides, and both Muwatalli and Ramesses claimed victory.

After the Battle of Kadesh, Muwatalli continued to expand into Syria, while the Egyptians had to stop their planned expansion. Because of this, it is believed that the Battle of Kadesh had significantly reduced Egypt's army, meaning they were incapable of continuing their military campaign. Historians agree that the Battle of Kadesh ended up in a draw, but the tactical victory belongs to Egypt. Ramesses II managed to avoid being captured or killed in an ambush, and the innovation of using lighter and faster two-men chariots gave him a slight advantage.

Muwatalli II continued to conquer as far south as the Egyptian province of Upi. He captured these lands and gave them to his brother Hattusili to rule. Egyptian influence was then reduced to Canaan only (today's Israel), and even there, a rebellion started. Ramesses II had to start a series of military campaigns in order to stop major uprisings from happening.

It took another fifteen years and a few more conflicts between the Hittites and the Egyptians before they finally signed a peace treaty, which would later be known in history as the Eternal Treaty. Before that happened, though, King Muwatalli II died in 1272 and was succeeded by his son, Mursili III. But he only reigned for about seven years, as he was deposed by his uncle, Hattusili, who became Hattusili III, and Mursili III fled the Hittite Empire, seeking refuge in Egypt. Hattusili demanded Ramesses II to deliver his nephew to him, but Ramesses claimed he didn't know Mursili's whereabouts. War almost broke out between the Hittites and the Egyptians over this dispute, but Ramesses decided to pursue an agreement with Hattusili. The document both sides signed is the first peace treaty known in history. It was written in two languages, Egyptian hieroglyphs and Akkadian. What is interesting about this fact is that one version is not simply a translation of the other. The wording is completely different, and while the Hittite version claims the Egyptians begged for peace, the other one claims it was the Hittites who did so. The treaty was concluded in 1258 BCE, and it contains eighteen articles that call for peace and describe how the gods themselves demand peace between Egypt and the Hittite Empire. One of the terms of this peace treaty was the marriage of Ramesses and one of the Hittite princesses. Hattusili chose his own daughter, Maathorneferure, for this role.

It is believed that Ramesses and Hattusili both wanted peace because of the growing threat the Assyrians posed. While the Egyptians and the Hittites were occupied with their own conflict, the Assyrian king, Shalmaneser I, expanded his kingdom into Anatolia, Babylonia, ancient Iran, Aram (Syria), Canaan, and Phoenicia. Assyria became a big threat to the trading routes of the Hittites, just as much as Egypt was.

Hattusili's son, Tudhaliya IV, was the last strong king of the Hittite Empire who was able to keep the Assyrians from fully occupying his lands, though he did lose a great deal of territory to them. However, he was defeated in the Battle of Nihriya in 1230 against Assyrian King Tukulti-Nnruta I. This battle is regarded as the peak of hostilities between the Assyrians and Hittites. After the battle, Tudhaliya IV had to fight to regain authority over his own kingdom, but he managed to stop any internal revolts from spreading. The Hittites and Assyrians fought for another five years before they finally negotiated peace.

The last known king of the Hittite Empire was Suppiluliuma II, son of Tudhaliya IV. He ruled between 1207 and 1178 BCE and is known for commanding a fleet that defeated the Cypriots, the native people of Cyprus. This is the first recorded naval battle known to historians. It is believed that Suppiluliuma II commanded a fleet of Ugaritic ships, named after a port in Syria. The records of his time report a major political instability in the Hittite Empire, as

Suppiluliuma had to fight the former vassal states of the empire, which lasted for the entire duration of his reign.

His predecessors had returned Hattusa to the status of being a capital city, but Suppiluliuma decided to abandon it once more, thus inducing the end of the Hittite Empire. Hattusa was burned to the ground around 1180 in a series of combined attacks by the Kaskas, Phrygians, and Bryges. Their enemies took advantage of this weakened Hittite Empire and ransacked its lands. Much of the Hittite territory was soon taken by the Assyrians, and thus, the great Hittite Empire ceased to exist.

Although the Hittite Empire didn't exist anymore, by 1160 BCE, a number of small successor Hittite kingdoms emerged. The most well known are Carchemish and Milid, but none of these new kingdoms ever reached the former glory of the empire. Eventually, even these Neo-Hittite kingdoms fell under the Neo-Assyrian Empire, which fully assimilated them somewhere between 722 and 705 BCE.

Chapter 2 – The Aramean Confederation

The Arameans were a tribal confederation of Northwest Semitic people. Their origin is found in the Aram region in today's Syria, which includes Aleppo. This region was known under the name Amurru from 2335 to 1750 BCE. During the Neo-Assyrian Empire, the Neo-Babylonian Empire, the Achaemenid Empire, which combined spanned between 911 and 330 BCE, Aram was referred to as Eber-Nari.

The Arameans never had an empire or even one great kingdom. They were, in fact, an alliance of small, independent kingdoms that were spread all around the Near East. These kingdoms occupied the territories of today's Syria, Lebanon, Israel, and parts of the Arabian Peninsula and south-central Turkey.

The Arameans appear for the first time in history during the Bronze Age Collapse (1200 to 900 BCE). What caused the abrupt collapse remains unknown; however, many historians believe that it was a turbulent event. This collapse caused a movement of people across the Middle East, Asia Minor, the Caucasus, North Africa, Iran,

Greece, and the Balkans. New tribes and peoples emerged from these movements.

The first reference to the Arameans can be found in an inscription of the Assyrian king Tiglath-Pileser I (ruled 1114 to 1076 BCE). This inscription mentions the conquering of the Ahlamu-Aramaeans, but soon after, this term was replaced with just Arameans in other Assyrian scripts. This is evidence that the Arameans were a dominant force amongst the nomadic peoples. They established themselves in Syria by the 12th century BCE but were subjugated by the Middle Assyrian Empire.

After the death of the Assyrian king Ashur-bel-kala in 1056, the Arameans gained their independence and pressed against the northern Assyrian border in hordes. During the late 11th century, they took complete control over the lands of Eber-Nari, and from this point, the region was referred to as Aramea. The Aramean kingdoms included Aram-Damascus, Hamath, Bit Adini, Bit Bahiani, Aram-Bet Rehob, and many more, as well as tribal polities such as Gambulu, Litau, and Puqudu.

The Arameans are mentioned in the Bible as well, which tells us that Saul, David, and Solomon, the biblical kings of Israel and Judah, fought against them during the 11th and 10th centuries BCE. Also, the biblical Book of Judges claims that Israel was under Aramean rule for eight years during the early 11th century. The same source mentions Othniel, the first of the biblical judges, who defeated the Aramean forces under the command of Chushan-rishathaim, the king of Aram-Naharaim, or northwest Mesopotamia. While the biblical sources aren't considered entirely accurate, and they are often difficult to prove, they do offer some historical insight on the Arameans, of which very little is factually known.

During this same period, in the north, the Arameans took control over the Neo-Hittite city-state of Hamath, which lies on the Orontes River. However, soon after, they separated themselves from the Indo-European Neo-Hittite kingdom. The Arameans also conquered

Sam'al, a Luwian-speaking Neo-Hittite territory, which soon after became an Aramean kingdom called Bit Agushi. This kingdom encompassed the territories from Arpad (northwestern Syria) to Aleppo. At this time, the Arameans were also moving to the east of the Euphrates. There they came in such large numbers that the territory was renamed to Aram-Naharaim, which means "Aram of the two rivers." Some of the eastern Aramean tribes settled in Babylonia, where one of their own was crowned as king of Babylon. He was known under the name of Adad-apla-iddina, but he was considered a usurper.

The Aramean and Assyrian armies often fought in the period between 1050 and 911 BCE. However, the Assyrians had to keep their trade routes open; therefore, they had to send several military expeditions into Aramea, Babylonia, Iran, and Asia Minor. Ultimately, the Aramean kingdoms were conquered by the Assyrians. This conquest started with the Neo-Assyrian king Adad-nirari II in 911, who fought off the Arameans attacking his borders and started a new expansion of the Assyrian Empire in all directions. Assyrian King Ashurnasirpal II and his son, Shalmaneser II, continued destroying the numerous Aramean tribes and managed to conquer the whole territory of Aramea. In addition, King Tiglath-Pileser III conquered Aram-Damascus in 732. The Assyrians changed the name of the Aramean kingdoms they conquered, but in Scripture, they were always referred to as Arameans. Furthermore, they forced deportation on the Arameans, thus moving them to Babylonia and Assyria, which already had small Aramean colonies. The result of this deportation was the birth of the Eastern Aramean dialect, which later became the common language in the entire Neo-Assyrian Empire, including Babylonia. A form of this language still survives to this day amongst indigenous Assyrian Christians in Iraq, Syria, Turkey, and Iran.

After the fall of the Neo-Assyrian Empire in 609, Aramea was ruled by the Neo-Babylonian Empire (626 to 539 BCE). The regions of the Aramean people became a battleground for the wars Babylon fought against Egypt. Even after the fall of Babylonia and throughout the later rule of the Persians, the Aramean region kept its name Eber Nari, and imperial Aramaic was still the official state language. It was during the Seleucid Empire that the name of the Aramean region was changed to Assyria. This name was commonly used to refer to the Assyrians and to the Arameans west of Aram, even though these two peoples were separate ethnically and historically. This name controversy is present even in modern times, as scholars cannot agree on the origin of the name of Syria. Today, most scholars agree that Assyria and Syria have the same etymological origins and that Syria is actually derived from Assyria.

Chapter 3 – The Luwians

Extent of the Luwians

Even though the Old Hittite Kingdom laws from the 17th century BCE mention the lands of Luwiya, there is no evidence for a unified state of Luwians or even a polity. When we speak about the Luwians, we speak about a group of people who spoke the common Luwian language of Indo-European origin and who were most likely a nomadic or semi-nomadic group of people. The origin of the Luwians remains a mystery. Perhaps they came from the Balkan regions or from the territories of the Lower Volga. However, we do know that they settled in the southern and western parts of Anatolia and that most likely their political center was in Purushanda, an ancient city-state. Purushanda has not yet been discovered, but we know of its existence from Cappadocian texts and Hittite texts discovered in Kanesh (central Turkey). From these texts, it is known that there was a king ruling in Purushanda and that he defended the city against the Hittite invasion led by King Anitta. The Hittites won and gave Purushanda the status of a privileged vassal state. But soon after, Purushanda was absorbed into the Hittite Empire and was no longer mentioned under that name again.

The Luwian language and hieroglyphic inscriptions were used throughout the history of the Middle and New Kingdoms of the Hittites. The kings in Hattusa used Luwian hieroglyphic inscriptions, and this system of writing was used even after the fall of the Neo-Hittite states and into the Neo-Assyrian Empire. It is impossible to conclude anything about the extent of Luwian lands based on the use of their inscriptions, but it is clear that the Luwian culture was present in ancient Anatolia. However, Luwian writing and their language are not enough to define their ethnicity. In this context, the Luwians are all the peoples that spoke the Luwian language, regardless of their ethnicity. It is important to make a distinction between Luwian and Hittite languages. Even though the Luwian language and inscriptions were present within the Hittite Empire, this does not make the Hittites a Luwian people. In fact, the Hittites had their own everyday language, also of Indo-European origin, which was officially known as Nesite, after the city Nesa, i.e., Kanesh.

Old Assyrian Empire documents from 1950 to 1700 BCE support the theory that the Luwians and Hittites spoke two different languages. In these documents, Luwian personal names and names of places appear for the first time. The Assyrians also borrowed many Luwian words and used them in their everyday language.

There are preserved Luwian religious texts that provide us with the knowledge of their culture, but they were inserted into Hittite documents and offer no insight into the Luwian people's history or origin. Everything known about the Luwian people is derived mostly from Hittite documents. There are some exceptions, though, such as correspondences between Egypt and Arzawa during the reign of Pharaoh Amenhotep III or the mention of the Lukka people, a group of people that spoke Luwian and settled in southwestern Anatolia, in correspondences between the king of Alasiya and Pharaoh Amenhotep IV. There is no strong evidence that supports any fact of the Luwian people's history, states, or political development. However, it is worth taking note that the Hittite reports do mention some dynastic quarrels and coups amongst the Luwian people, but no details were given as they did not involve the Hittite Empire directly.

The Hittites saw the Luwians as enemies, or at least as potential enemies occupying strategically important lands. They even went to the extent of describing one of the Arzawan vassal rulers as a treacherous, disloyal subject, which makes historians wonder whether he was a hero to the Luwians, as he fought for independence from their Hittite overlords. However, at this point, everything is just speculation as there are no Luwian or Arzawan texts that survived. Even when it comes to the correspondence letter between the Hittites and Arzawa lands, only the Hittite letters survived, or rather copies of the letters survived.

In western Anatolia, there were five states, or kingdoms, occupying the region known as the Arzawa lands. This region was populated by large numbers of Luwian-speaking peoples. The initial Luwian appearance in Anatolia may be due to migration through the northwestern regions, which would explain the early settlements in the Arzawan lands and establishments of a number of small kingdoms. These five kingdoms were known as Arzawa Minor, Mira, the Seha River Land, Wilusa, and Hapalla. The history of these kingdoms is known from surviving Hittite texts, amongst them a treaty from the 13th century BCE between the king of the Hittites, Muwatalli II, and the king of Wilusa, Alaksandu. Since the Arzawa lands entered Hittite documents under this name, the term Luwiya suddenly disappears from the records.

Once the Hittites conquered all of the Arzawan lands, four of the five Arzawa kingdoms became vassal states of the Hittite Empire. Arzawa Minor is not even mentioned in this treaty drawn by Muwatalli II, which is most likely due to this state being completely dismembered during the war campaigns led by King Mursili II. After two years of fighting, Arzawa Minor was probably destroyed, and a large piece of it was claimed by the Kingdom of Mira. Deep in the lands of Arzawa Minor, there is a statue depicting a king of Mira named Tarkasnawa, who ruled in the 13th century.

A number of Hittite texts, as well as some Egyptian documents, mention the Lukka people. But these texts do not mention any political or administrative organization amongst these people. There is no evidence of Lukka kings ever existing, and no Lukka state has ever existed by that name. It is possible that while the Arzawa lands were forming their smaller states, certain populations wanted to maintain their independence and therefore resisted the newly created kingdoms. This might be how a group of Luwian people, united under the name Lukka, attracted the attention of the Hittite Empire. Hittite documents state that the Lukka people became subjects of the Hittite kings after they spread their empire across the territories of Arzawa. The impression these Hittite documents leave is that the Lukka people were hostile toward their new king and were not easily controlled. They are also mentioned as seafarers, often indulging in buccaneering campaigns against Mediterranean coastal cities. In Hittite documents, there is also a mention of Lukka lands, which leads to the conclusion that the Lukka region did exist, at least as a place that they could call a homeland, as they were scattered throughout southern and western Anatolia. Historians presume this Lukka homeland must include at least part of the coastline, as we have evidence they were seafarers. A probable territory that could fall under the Lukka homeland is a western region of the Taurus Mountains and its rugged coast, which later became the country of Lycia (now known as the provinces of Antalya and Mugla in Turkey). It is even possible that the Greek name for this region, Lycia, is directly derived from the Bronze Age name Lukka. A bronze tablet discovered in Hattusa offers further evidence of this region being known as Lukka. It is a treaty document from the 13th century drawn up by Hittite King Tudhaliya IV. In terms of borders, this treaty mentions the city of Parha (later known as Perga), a name which was in other documents used in the same context as the Lukka lands.

The first mention of the Arzawan lands are found in records about the raids led by Hittite King Hattusili I. He records his various military campaigns in a span of six years, and in the third year, he notes taking cattle and sheep from the Arzawan lands. Hattusili is known for his war campaigns against Syria and eastern Anatolia, and it is very interesting that he even recorded a raid to the west, which only had the purpose of plundering. This recorded raid was probably not the only one, as it was more likely that there were a number of such raids on neighboring Arzawan lands, which alludes to further Hittite expansion at the expense of the Luwians. An early text from the palace chronicles suggests that during the rule of King Hattusili I, part of the Arzawan territories fell under the rule of the Hittite kingdom. This text speaks of a city called Hurma and its surrounding regions, which are known to be part of the Arzawan lands.

The first solid records that shed some light on Hittite-Arzawa relations come from King Tudhaliya I's annals. Two military campaigns are recorded in these annals, both under the direct leadership of King Tudhaliya himself. The first campaign was against several countries, including Arzawa Minor, the Seha River Land, and Hapalla. All three states are identified as Luwian lands. The annals speak of the victory King Tudhaliya won in the first military campaign against the western kingdoms, but shortly after, he had to reorganize his military forces for further actions in the same region. In his second campaign, the king encountered resistance in the form of an anti-Hittite coalition, which numbered 22 nations. Wilusa, a Luwian state, is also mentioned in the texts that refer to the second military campaign. The coalition was defeated, however, and the Hittites were victorious. It is not known whether the coalition or one similar to it was ever formed again.

Even though the Hittites won and destroyed the coalition, they did not establish a permanent authority in the Arzawan lands. The Luwians probably managed to keep their independence since there is no evidence of the western kingdoms becoming Hittite vassals. Tudhaliya I was probably just trying to pacify a region that presented a threat to his kingdom. The Hittites needed peace on their western borders so they could concentrate on their military expansion in the north and southeast.

A document known as the *Indictment of Madduwatta* offers more information about Arzawa-Hittite relations. This document reveals that Madduwatta, the king of Arzawa (ruled in the 14th or 13th century) was exiled from his lands, somewhere in western Anatolia, and that he sought refuge with King Tudhaliya I. He was accompanied by his family and military troops with chariots, which is a sign of his importance. Tudhaliya gave him the lands of Zippasla to rule as a vassal king, but later on, he expanded Madduwatta's new kingdom by including the Siyanta River Lands. It is unclear where Madduwatta's kingdom was, but the documents describe it as being on the periphery of the Arzawan lands. Tudhaliya instructed Madduwatta not to try to expand his kingdom, but Madduwatta was quick to violate this agreement, and he attempted to conquer parts of the Arzawan lands ruled by Kupanta-Kurunta. Madduwatta's army was destroyed, but Kupanta-Kurunta wasn't satisfied just with defending his territory. He launched a counterattack on Madduwatta's kingdom, forcing him to flee. Tudhaliya came to help and drove Kupanta-Kurunta back to his own lands. He then restored Madduwatta as a vassal king, giving him the spoils of war. It is unknown why Tudhaliya was so generous toward his vassal when he obviously violated the agreement and tried to expand his lands. Soon after, Madduwatta concluded a peace treaty with Kupanta-Kurunta, giving him his own daughter as a bride. In correspondence with an unsatisfied Tudhaliya, he explained this peace was just a trick in a larger scheme devised to kill Kupanta-Kurunta. This is where the text becomes fragmented, so it is not known what happened next and how these affairs ended.

These texts are clearly filled with a bias toward the Hittites, but they do offer insight into Hittite-Arzawa relations. They reveal Arzawa as being an independent land under the rule of Kupanta-Kurunta, who was hostile toward the Hittite Empire. It is believed that he was the king of Arzawa Minor because it is the only Arzawa state close to the western border of the Hittite Empire while adjoining Madduwatta's vassal state of Zippasla.

Hapalla was the only Arzawan land the Hittite Empire claimed sovereignty over. Madduwatta tried to take Hapalla for his own kingdom; however, Hittite King Arnuwanda I did not approve of this, and he asked Madduwatta to return it. Madduwatta didn't want to antagonize his Hittite overlord, but he did take and keep some other lands that might have been of interest to Arnuwanda. Some of these were well within the Lukka territory.

In the Late Bronze Age, the Luwians were the largest population in Anatolia. They were also rapidly spreading their influence over western and southern Anatolia. They even formed kingdoms in the west, joined various alliances, and had a significant army at their disposal. However, they were the enemies of the Hittite Empire, with Arzawa Minor being the most influential in this hostility. It was also the largest kingdom led by Kupanta-Kurunta, who entered into conflict with the Hittites twice, and even though he lost both times, he did succeed in occupying some of the Hittite vassal states. His actions were a clear sign to the Hittite kings that Arzawa Minor would constantly pose a threat to their plans of expansion to the west.

At one point in history, Arzawa Minor had an opportunity of becoming a major power in Anatolia. During the reign of Tudhaliya III, the Hittite kingdom was invaded and sacked. Arzawa joined the invaders and attacked the Hittites from the southwest. Even the capital of Hattusa was sacked during this invasion, and the royal family had to seek shelter in the temporary stronghold of Samuha. These events opened a way for Arzawa Minor to become a dominant power in Anatolia. The Arzawan ruler Tarhuntaradu was observed as the next Great King of Anatolia, even by the Egyptian pharaoh Amenhotep III, who asked him for one of his daughters in marriage. But under the new king Suppiluliuma I, the Hittites managed to drive the usurpers from their lands and also set a goal of destroying Arzawa. His first task was to defeat the Arzawan troops in the Lower Land, from where they attacked the Hittite kingdom in the first place, and even though he succeeded, Arzawa remained a constant threat to the borders of the Hittite kingdom for as long as Suppiluliuma ruled.

The Arzawan leader Anzapahhaddu at one point gave asylum to some Hittite refugees but refused to deliver them back to Suppiluliuma. Under the command of a certain Himuili, the Hittite forces were tasked with retrieving refugees, but Anzapahhaddu defeated them, forcing Suppiluliuma to come out on the battlefield and give in to his demands.

During these upheavals with Arzawa Minor, Hapalla managed to finally gain independence from the Hittite kingdom. However, Suppiluliuma appointed his most able commander, Hannutti, as the new governor of the Lower Lands, and he launched an attack on Hapalla in hopes of restoring it to Hittite sovereignty. After Hannutti's army plundered Hapalla of its livestock and people, it was once again restored under Hittite rule.

The Arzawan lands were becoming a constant burden on the southwestern border of the Hittite Empire, and it was just a matter of time until they had to be dealt with. However, the Hittite throne was now occupied by a young and inexperienced king, Mursili II, who was crowned after his father's and brother's sudden death due to the plague. His empire was drowning in rebellions, and he received threats of war from neighboring kingdoms who thought him to be too incompetent to rule. After two years of pacification campaigns throughout his own kingdom, and after dealing with the Kaska rebellion in the north, Arzawa Minor drew its attention to the west. Under the leadership of Uhhaziti, Arzawa Minor became an instigator of an anti-Hittite movement in the region. Uhhaziti was a king in Arzawa Minor and an ally to Mursili's father, Suppiluliuma, but he turned against the Hittites when Mursili II became its king. Uhhaziti allied himself with the king of Ahhiyawa, a kingdom of mainland Greece that possibly had the city of Mycenae as its seat of power. The state of Millawanda (classically known as Miletus) joined this alliance, and it was probably this act that made Mursili act against Millawanda, as it was then conquered by the Hittites.

However, this did not stop Uhhaziti in his anti-Hittite campaigns. He mocked the Hittite king, calling him a child, and instigating a war. Mursili's brother, Sharri-Kushuh, the viceroy of Carchemish, joined the fight, which lasted for two years. The deciding battle took place at the Astarpa River in Walma, a natural border of the Hittite Empire and the Arzawan lands. Mursili won against Arzawa's king and pursued his army to the city of Apasa, which he took without any resistance. However, he failed to capture King Uhhaziti, who managed to escape the city. Puranda was the last city to be conquered, and with its fall, the Arzawan resistance was officially dealt with.

Only one Arzawan kingdom remained a potential threat, and that was the Seha River Land. It is unclear whether they were already a vassal state of the Hittite Empire, but what is certain from surviving documents is that the king of the Seha River Land, Manapa-Tarhunta, owed his position to the Hittite Empire, as they had backed him when he fought his brothers for kingship. Later, he turned against Mursili, helping Uhhaziti in his rebellion instead. However, when Mursili threatened to attack, Manapa-Tarhunta begged Mursili to spare his people. Initially, Mursili refused and came close to the city gates, where the king's mother begged him again to spare them. The Seha River Land were taken without any further resistance, and from this point on, they officially became a vassal state. Mursili II managed to take over all of the Arzawan lands and turned them into vassal states to the Hittite Empire. After the fall of Puranda and the death of King Uhhaziti, who died in exile, there is no mention of Arzawa Minor as a separate state, at least under that name, which leads to the conclusion that this was the point when it ceased to exist.

The peace after Mursili II claimed Arzawa Minor did not last long. From Kupanta-Kurunta's treaty (not to be confused with Arzawa King Kupanta-Kurunta, it is evident that in Mursili's twelfth year of rule, he, once again, had to turn his forces to the west and deal with an uprising in the Luwian lands. This uprising was led by a man of unknown origin. Mashuiluwa, the king of Mira, who was previously loyal to the Hittite Empire, joined this rebellion. Mursili turned west and brought an army, but he still called Mashuiluwa to appear before him, probably hoping to avoid open war. However, Mashuiluwa decided to run and seek sanctuary in the land of Masa. Mursili asked the authorities of Masa for his deliverance, and they obliged. Mashuiluwa was exiled from his own kingdom, but he was given a permanent residence in Hattusa.

After their king fled, the people of Mira took a pro-Hittite stand, and the nobles officially dissociated themselves from Mashuiluwa's actions. Mursili granted the throne of Mira to Kupanta-Kurunta, Mashuiluwa's nephew, but he also had support from the nobility. After this episode, there is no more evidence of uprisings or rebellions in the Arzawan lands during the rest of the rule of King Mursili II. Mursili was succeeded by his son, Muwatalli II, whose first years of rule were also free of Luwian unrests.

The peace in western Anatolia lasted approximately for two decades. A new round of unrest, which started around 1280, suggested the involvement of a highborn man named Piyamaradu, who started building a new power base in the regions of the Hittite vassal states. At this time, Millawanda was under Ahhiyawa's control, and so, Piyamaradu joined forces with the Ahhiyawan king. The result of this alliance was that Piyamaradu somehow gained control over Wilusa.

It is known that Wilusa was a Luwian kingdom in northwestern Anatolia, a landmass that geographically is in the vicinity of Troy. A Swiss scholar, Emil Forrer, who lived during the 1920s, started a debate that stated that linguistically Wilusa and another Arzawa state, Taruisa, are similar. This statement caused debate that is still ongoing amongst historians, but the majority now agrees that evidence identifying Wilusa as Iliad is not to be ignored. This could very well mean that Trojans between the 17th and 15th century BCE were, in fact, a Luwian-speaking group of people, as well as perhaps their predecessors.

Piyamaradu was soon after defeated and removed from Wilusa. A legitimate king, Alaksandu, was now on the throne, and he returned it to become a vassal state of the Hittite Empire once more. Piyamaradu himself managed to escape being captured by the Hittites, most likely seeking refuge with the Ahhiyawan king. He remained an anti-Hittite propagator in western Anatolia for many years to come. Piyamaradu was actually linked to Kupanta-Kurunta in Mira, but surviving texts are insufficient to indicate what their relation was. At this time, Mira was a loyal vassal state to Muwatalli's Hittite Empire, and most likely, they were hostile toward Piyamaradu.

Muwatalli was succeeded by his son, Mursili III, who had to fight a civil war with his uncle Hattusili. This war had a destabilizing effect on the entire Hittite Empire and very likely involved the western vassal states occupied by the Luwians. The king of the Seha River Land supported Hattusili, but the kings of other Arzawan lands remained loyal to Mursili III, amongst them being Kupanta-Kurunta. Hattusili won the civil war and gained the throne before any of the vassal states were directly involved in the conflict. The only surviving document regarding the Luwian lands that is not of Hittite origin is a letter Pharaoh Ramesses II sent to Kupanta-Kurunta. This letter was obviously a reply to a non-surviving letter of Kupanta-Kurunta in which he asked Ramesses whether he supported Hattusili or Mursili. Ramesses' response was probably the reason why Kupanta-Kurunta chose to stay loyal to the Hittite Empire, as the pharaoh was in open support of Hattusili.

During the same period, in southeast Anatolia, there were also great numbers of Luwian-speaking people. Stretching along the Mediterranean coast and farther inland, they are known as the Kizzuwatna and Tarhuntassa (see the map at the beginning of this chapter for reference). From the plain of Adana to the Anti-Taurus Mountains, covering a region of classical Cilicia, laid Kizzuwatna. It had cult centers in the cities of Kummanni and Lawanatiya. Other known cities of the Kizzuwatna territories were Sinuwanda, Zunnahara, Arana, and Sinahu. The two dominant groups of people in this region were the Luwians and the Hurrians, although there may have been a small Semitic community presence as well. A mixture of personal names in Kizzuwatna suggests the mixture of Luwian and Hurrian cultures throughout these territories. The first known Hittite treaty was with Kizzuwatna's king, Iputahsu. Their successors also drew up treaties, which suggest that there were frequent conflicts between the Hittites and Kizzuwatna. The conflicts involved the sacking and even destruction of border cities on both the Hittite and Kizzuwatna territories.

Kizzuwatna was on the main communication route with Syria, and its strategic importance made the Hittites willing to work on a permanent alliance. However, Kizzuwatna often switched sides, as they were also threatened by the Hurrian kingdom of Mitanni and their vassal king, Idrimi of Alalakh. During the reign of the Hittite king Tudhaliya I, Kizzuwatna's King Sunassura signed a treaty that would permanently bind them to the Hittite Empire.

Tarhuntassa, another region that was occupied by a Luwian-speaking people, adjoined Kizzuwatna to the west. Its name is purely Luwian, as it suggests the Luwian storm god Tarhunt. The existence of this kingdom was first noted during the reign of the Hittite king Muwatalli II. It also seems to have been created by Muwatalli himself, who incorporated the Hulaya River Land in its territory. This kingdom was given to Kurunta, the second son of Muwatalli, to rule. Because of its strategic location, Tarhuntassa played a great role in the final decades of the Hittite Empire. It is believed that the port of Ura was within its borders, if not next to Tarhuntassa, and it was this port that ships from Egypt brought grain to the Hittite Empire. It was of great importance to keep the port city of Ura away from hostile territories. A hieroglyphic inscription discovered in Hattusa suggests that during the reign of Suppiluliuma II, the conquest of southern Anatolia occurred, and Tarhuntassa was annexed. This means that, at that time, Tarhuntassa had a policy of being hostile to the Hittites.

During the Late Bronze Age, the Luwian people were dispersed all around Anatolia. They were constantly moving, as they lived a nomadic life; however, they were also forcefully moved by the Hittites, who waged wars against them and captured them as slaves and workers throughout the Hittite territories. As a result of the war campaigns of Tudhaliya I, Suppiluliuma I, and Mursili II, there must have been thousands of Luwians in the Hittite lands when the Hittite New Kingdom ended. Because of the Luwians' nomadic nature and their slave/worker status within the Hittite kingdom, they probably mostly inhabited the peripheral farm territories of the Hittite homeland. The Luwians quickly assimilated to the new Hittite culture, but the Hittites had a policy of incorporating all the new gods of conquered peoples into their own pantheon. Thus, the Luwian culture survived in one of its shapes, namely religion, which had an impact on Hittite cultural development.

However, the Hittites had little to no cultural influence on their newly conquered western lands. Arzawa was mainly under Mycenaean and Minoan Greek influence, especially during the late 14th century.

From Hattusili III's Tawagalawa letter, it is evident that the Mycenaean world had a substantial number of Luwians. Hattusili complains how around 7,000 Luwians from the Lukka lands had been transported to Ahhiyawa as a labor force for construction, the textile industry, and domestic service. Aside from being a labor force, the Mycenaeans were also interested in the raw materials western Anatolia had to offer. During the Late Bronze Age, Anatolia was rich in timber, copper, gold, and silver, and these were, undoubtedly, the items that attracted the Mycenaeans to Anatolia in the first place.

An inscription on the wall of the temple of Karnak (Luxor, Egypt) speaks of the Luwian "sea-people" who attacked the Nile Delta during the reign of Ramesses II's son Merneptah (ruled 1213 to 1204). The names mentioned in this inscription are Sherden, Shekelesh, Ekwesh, Lukka, and Teresh. The linguistics of these names suggests they were all Luwian-speaking peoples, and since the mention of Lukka is amongst them, it practically confirms this theory. This invasion was considered to be just a prelude to the great invasion of the Sea Peoples. The magnitude of this invasion was witnessed by the territories they passed through, and there were many of them. The mentioned destroyed lands include Arzawa, Hatti, Qode (possibly Cilicia), Carchemish, and Alasiya. Looking at the list of kingdoms, it is evident that the spread of the Sea Peoples extended across nearly the entire Near East.

After the fall of the Hittite Empire, the Luwian people and the elements of Luwian culture survived through the centuries. The Luwians had a strong influence on the kingdoms that developed on the territories that used to belong to the once great Hittite Empire. These elements mostly appear in the southern regions of Anatolia. The Luwian names throughout the southern regions of Anatolia in the first millennium BCE indicate their existence up to the Hellenistic and Roman imperial periods. These onomastic elements of Luwian origin are found in the documents of Lucia, Pisidia, Pamphylia, Isauria, Lycaonia, and Cilicia. Cilicia Aspera (Tracheia) and Lycia are two regions where Luwian names are concentrated in great numbers. Because of this concentration of names, the conclusion is that these were the centers of Luwian occupation in southern Anatolia after the fall of the Neo-Hittite kingdoms. Both of these regions are mountainous and are not easily approachable by land or by sea. This isolation might be what offered the opportunity for the Luwian people to survive the various upheavals and foreign intrusions during the Late Bronze Age. But this isolation had its drawbacks in a historical sense. The Luwians who inhabited the mountainous regions are rarely mentioned in surviving texts and documents. With the exception of those names, nothing else survived; therefore, historians lack concrete details about these people.

Surviving local inscriptions in Lycia are evidence enough that this region was mainly inhabited by Luwian-speaking people for the first six centuries of the Iron Age. But Cilicia Aspera has no such surviving inscriptions. However, similarities in names used in Lycia and Cilicia may lead us to the conclusion that Cilicia was also inhabited by a large population of Luwians. Cilicia was divided into two parts, Cilicia Aspera, which encompassed the mountainous regions, and Cilicia Campestris, the fertile plains in the east. In Cilicia Campestris, a Phoenician hieroglyphic bilingual inscription was found. It appears at the north and south gates of the fortification of Karatepe-Aslantas. The inscription was commissioned by a local ruler named Azatiwada, who claimed to have brought peace to the land of Adana and that it was he who established the royal family on the throne. In the same inscription, Azatiwada mentions the name of Muksa, which historians believe to be a Luwian seer called Mopsos, who was the leader of the Luwian people who emigrated from western Anatolia to Cilicia. Azatiwada mentioned that Muksa is also the founder of the ruling family in Cilicia.

Lycia, a country in southwestern Anatolia, is the best example of Luwian presence in the first millennium BCE. Lycia is, in fact, a region that was called Lukka lands in Hittite texts and documents.

This region remained unaffected by the fall of the kingdoms during the Late Bronze Age. It is speculated that the Lukka lands received Luwian refugees from other kingdoms that were a part of the Arzawan lands or other western Anatolian regions. Lycia was also surrounded by a mountainous region, which served as a natural isolating border that may have helped this territory to preserve its Luwian elements.

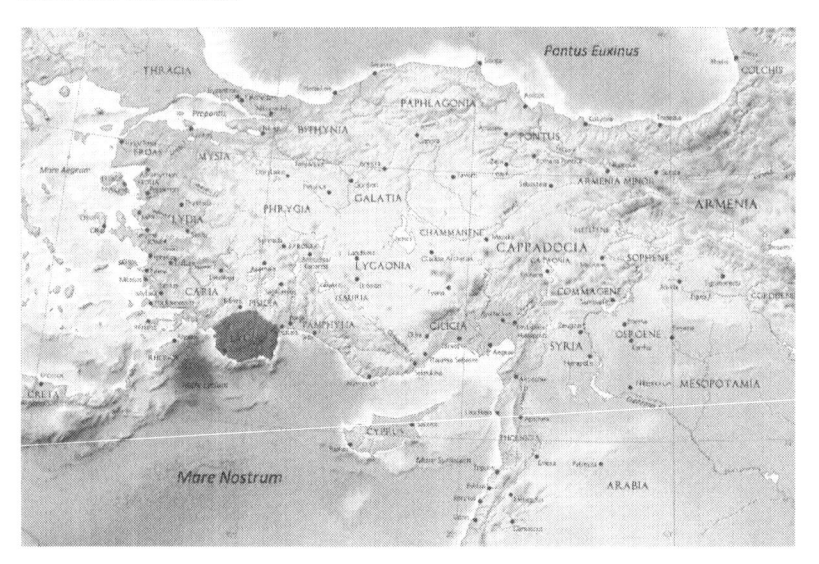

Anatolia in the Greco-Roman period

Lycia is the Greek name for the country first found in Homer's *Iliad*. However, the inhabitants of Lycia called their country Trmmisa. The Greek name is obviously a transcription of the Bronze Age name Lukka, although some historians have tried to explain the name using Hellenocentric evidence, claiming that the name Lycia is purely of Greek origin. As for the name Trmmisa, there might have been a strong political and cultural presence in Lycia of another group of people, possibly Cretan immigrants, who called themselves Trmmili. This would explain how the term became synonymous for all the peoples inhabiting the lands of Lycia.

Since Lycia was inhabited mainly by a Luwian-speaking people, it is presumed that they continued their nomadic way of life. This means that they were scattered throughout the mountains, pasturing herds and flocks during the hot summer months. However, there were a number of permanent settlements, mainly religious or political centers. The Xanthos valley was probably the main area for settlement in Lycia. The land there was fertile, rich in crops and orchards due to the River Xanthos, whose banks were an area for some of the very first settlements in this region.

Lycia appears for the first time in foreign texts, in Rhodes, to be specific, during the first millennium. It appears the Rhodians were hostile to Lycia. The Rhodians settled on the southern Anatolian coast, a region that would later become eastern Lycia. However, apart from conflicts with Rhodes, Lycia remained uninfluenced by other foreign powers, probably due to its isolation from the rest of Anatolia. Herodotus, an influential Greek historian who lived during the 5th century BCE, claimed that Lycia and Cilicia were the only lands that remained free of King Croesus of Lydia's occupation.

But in 540, Lycia finally succumbed to a foreign power. Harpagos, a Median general who worked for the Persians, campaigned in these regions, and he confronted a small Lycian army, which he easily defeated and then took over Xanthos. Herodotus writes that when the Lycians saw they were defeated, they gathered their wives, children, slaves, and all the property they could move inside Xanthos and burned it all to the ground. They made one last attack against the Persian army, but they were unsuccessful and were all killed. Lycia finally became a vassal state of the Persian Empire, and the city of Xanthos was rebuilt and repopulated. Around 516/515 BCE, the first ruling family was established in Xanthos, probably with great influence from the Persian Empire. Lycia became a loyal ally to the Persians until the fifth century when it became a part of the Delian League. However, Lycia broke away from this confederacy, probably during the Peloponnesian War, which started in 431. Soon after, it resumed its alliance with Persia. In 367, Lycia participated in a satrap rebellion against Persia, but this rebellion was crushed after nine years, and Lycia was once more the subject of the Persian

Empire, thus losing much of its autonomy. This new status didn't last long as in 334/3, Lycia was invaded by Alexander the Great and was never again under Persian rule.

Reconstructing the history of the Luwian-speaking groups of people proves to be a difficult task due to the lack of evidence. What is known about the regions they inhabited is mostly from inscriptions left by hostile neighbors. These inscriptions are also very biased and must be taken with an ounce of suspicion when it comes to their factual accuracy. The only texts that are originally Luwian are of religious nature, and they were inserted into Hittite documents. They do provide some evidence of Luwian culture, but there are no such texts that provide historical information of these people. The Luwians of the Bronze Age are mostly known from texts or correspondence between Hittite rulers, whose interests in the lands inhabited by the Luwians were limited.

The Hittites were a dominant force in Anatolia during the Bronze Age period, so it is known that the Luwians had a relationship with the Hittite Empire. They saw each other as enemies, or at least as potential threats to each other, and much of the surviving Hittite texts that concern the Luwian lands are propaganda against them.

After the Bronze Age, Luwian history is based on the assumption that the appearance of Luwian inscriptions means there was an actual presence of Luwian-speaking people in southern Anatolia. In fact, there is a big chance the Luwians were only a minority in these regions, as the dominant culture at the time was Hurrian. It is also known that the Luwian hieroglyphic system was adopted by other ethnicities as a simpler and more effective way of writing. The Hittites were the first to adopt Luwian hieroglyphs and replaced their own cuneiform script with it. This may as well have happened during the Early Iron Age, and therefore, the inscriptions found in Luwian might not be of actual Luwian origin at all.

A significant number of Luwian names in certain regions, as well as the usage of the Luwian hieroglyphic script, confirms the existence of Luwian-speaking populations, but they do not attest to any Luwian influence on culture or politics in these lands. On the other hand, we have a cluster of Luwian names in Cilicia and Lycia, but there's a lack of Luwian hieroglyphic inscriptions. This is why historians speak of the existence of Luwian elements rather than the Luwian people themselves. However, the change to a Hellenistic-oriented world might have had some influence on the choice of writing in southern Anatolia, and it might not have had anything to do with the existence, or non-existence, of Luwians in Cilicia and Lycia. The Luwian-based language was still in use in Lycia during the sixth to fourth century BCE when the Greek alphabet was in use. This is an indicator of an almost certain Luwian presence in Lycia.

Regarding Syria, there is no evidence of a Luwian-speaking people having a settlement there. Even though there are a number of inscriptions found in Syria that use Luwian hieroglyphs, they are of Neo-Hittite origin. Same as the title of "The Great King," the Luwian script was passed on amongst the royal families of the Neo-Hittite kingdoms. There may not be enough evidence of a Luwian settlement, but the use of the Luwian script speaks of the magnitude of their influence on ancient Anatolia.

Chapter 4 – The Neo-Assyrian Empire

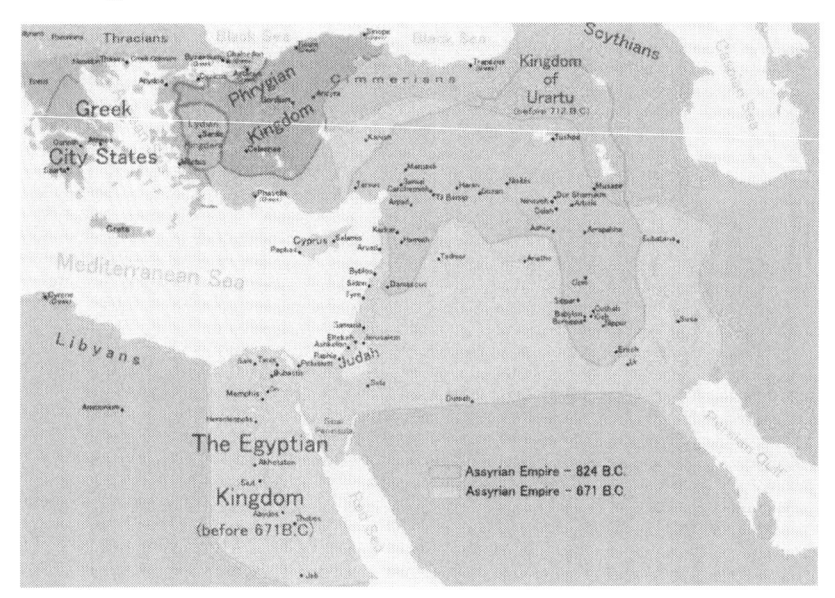

Map of Neo-Assyrian Empire

The Neo-Assyrian Empire was the largest empire in the world during the period known as the Iron Age. It lasted from 911 until 609 BCE and succeeded the Old (2025 to 1378) and Middle (1365 to 934) Assyrian Empires of the Bronze Age. Its official language was

Aramaic, but many other languages were common, including Hittite, Hurrian, Egyptian, and Phoenician. This is due to the Assyrian practice of relocating the people of newly conquered territories to the old nucleus of the empire.

During its height, the Neo-Assyrian Empire spread from the Zagros Mountains in the east to the Levant (today's Syria-Palestine) and a large part of Egypt to the west, and from the Persian Gulf to the south to the source of the Tigris and Euphrates in Anatolia. This massive territory is what made the Neo-Assyrian Empire the largest empire that the Iron Age ever knew and also one of the most enduring since it lasted for around 300 years.

The first emperor of the Neo-Assyrian period was Ashur-dan II, who ruled between 934 and 912 BC. He began to reclaim and expand the territories of the Assyrian Empire, a practice that was embraced by his successors. His son, Adad-nirari II, was the one who ensured Assyria would be recognized as a great power in the known world. He led war campaigns against Egypt, where he managed to overthrow the Nubian dynasty. He then proceeded to conquer Elam, Urartu, Media, Persia, Canaan, Arabia, Israel, Judah, Samarra, Cilicia, Cyprus, Chaldea, and the Neo-Hittite states, among others. The Assyrians waged wars against their neighbors every year and had a well-organized, modern army for this period.

However, the Assyrians, in general, lagged behind other empires when it came to the usage of iron. The Hittites mastered the production of iron by the 13th century BCE, but Assyria only began using iron during the 9th century. Until then, it mostly relied on bronze for weapons and tools. Even between the 9th and 8th centuries, Assyria used only the iron obtained as spoils of war from the defeated Hittites. However, by the late 8th century, they began extracting it and working it themselves. This delay in iron use didn't affect Assyrian military success. In fact, many of the technological improvements and innovations of the Early Iron Age are attributed to the Assyrians. For instance, they were the ones who developed advanced chariots with a platform that could support three or even four men: a driver, bowman, and shield-bearer. In addition, they improved battering rams, invented earthen ramps, and employed sappers (combat engineers).

When it comes to the political structure of the Neo-Assyrian Empire, it relied on the heritage of the Middle Assyrian period. The king was regarded as someone who had an intimate relationship with the god Ashur, and he was the one who enforced the divine will. The kings had absolute power over the state and were also in charge of managing an efficient government. Furthermore, they were the ones who were responsible for the religious life of the empire and who had to provide the maintenance of shrines. However, in the Neo-Assyrian Empire, no formal legal code existed. The kings were the supreme legislators and chief justices. Most common legal matters were regulated by customs, but the king had the right to involve himself in any legal matter he thought would need his intervention.

The Assyrian kings were not regarded as immortals; instead, they were supreme human beings who were very much mortal. The kings were also the military leaders, as Assyria was a military state, but they didn't always lead the army in person. The army was usually led by priests carrying the statues of their gods in front of religious processions. For them, wars were religious actions, and they were always seen as the will of Ashur.

The administration of the empire made a clear distinction between the core Assyrian provinces, northern Mesopotamian provinces, which paid different taxes, and the vassal states of the Assyrian Empire, which had to pay a special tribute to the empire. Each province had a governor who was named by the king himself, while the vassal states had their own ruling families who were loyal to Assyria.

There is not enough information preserved about the everyday life of the common people. The majority of the population consisted of farmers and workers. Clans lived together in villages, taking care of the agricultural holdings in the vicinity. Each village had a mayor who was their representative before the state officials and who was also, in some cases, the local judge. There are no recorded rebellions of the common people against Assyrian rule. The only rebellions ever recorded were the ones of noble families fighting the empire. The state was the owner of everything that was produced; however, the king was responsible for providing the infrastructure, construction, and the expansion of agricultural lands, including trade, though trade sometimes employed private contractors. The state was the largest employer of labor, free people, semi-free people, and slaves.

The Bronze Age Collapse (1200 to 900 BCE), also known as the Dark Age of the Near East, did not affect the Middle Assyrian Empire for at least the next 150 years. While kingdoms crumbled around them, the Assyrians seemed to be completely unaffected. However, after the death of King Ashur-bel-kala in 1056, the decline of the empire began. During the span of just one century, Assyria lost all of its territories and ended up controlling only areas in the immediate vicinity of Assyria itself.

Semitic peoples, the Arameans, Chaldeans, and Suteans, inhabited the areas west and southwest of Assyria, including parts of Babylonia in the south. East of Assyria, the lands were inhabited by the Persians and Parthians. In the north, the Phrygians conquered the Neo-Hittite kingdoms. In eastern Anatolia, the Hurrians organized a new kingdom named Urartu. Even though Assyria lost all of its territories, at its heart, it remained a strong and stable state. This stability would allow Iron Age kings to retake all of their lost territories and expand their empire even more.

King Adad-nirari II (ruled 911 to 891 BCE) succeeded his father after some minor dynastic struggles. He is often considered to be the first king of the Neo-Assyrian Empire, but some historians argue that it was his father, Ashur-dan II.

Adad-nirari II started his rule with a military campaign to conquer the territories that already had the status of vassal states. In 910, at the junction of the Khabur and Euphrates Rivers, he defeated the Arameans. After taking their lands, he deported the Arameans, strategically making it impossible for them to cause any trouble in the future. Furthermore, he led regular military campaigns and conquered the Neo-Hittites and Hurrians in the north. He even attacked and defeated the Babylonian king Shamash-mudammiq twice, taking the lands and cities of central Mesopotamia. Later during his reign, he waged war against Babylonia's next king, Nabu-shuma-ukin I, and took even more territories. In the west, Adad-nirari conquered the Kabur River region as well as the Aramean cities of Kadmuh and Nisibin.

His son and successor was Tukulti-Ninurta II (ruled 891 to 884), who continued with the expansion of the Neo-Assyrian Empire by conquering lands in Asia Minor. His reign was short, but he confirmed Assyria's power in the region. He led a war campaign against the Aramean state of Bit-Zamani, forcing its king to sign a treaty that prohibited them from selling horses to Assyrian enemies. Bit-Zamani became an Assyrian ally with this treaty, but not much later, it gained the status a of vassal state. Tukulti-Ninurta II was known for developing the cities of Nineveh and Assur, and he also reinforced the city walls and built palaces, temples, and gardens.

After Tukulti-Ninurta, the throne was occupied by his son Ashurnasirpal II (ruled 883 to 859), whose reign was filled with conquests. He also started a very aggressive expansion program, which led to some revolts that were quickly crushed. Ashurnasirpal was known for being a brutal king who used war captives to build the new seat of power, a city called Nimrud, located in Mesopotamia. But he also added to the wealth of Assyria and invested considerably in art. Instead of depending on local rulers of the vassal states, Ashurnasirpal installed his own governors, thus gaining better control and even more power over the Assyrian Empire.

Ashurnasirpal campaigned against the Arameans and the Babylonians, just as his predecessors. However, his biggest accomplishment was the war against the Neo-Hittite states. Before his military campaign into the Hittite lands, Ashurnasirpal had to deal with a rebellion that occurred in 877 in the Middle Euphrates region. Apparently, the lands of Laqe, Hindanu, and Suhu broke their allegiance to the empire and formed a coalition that became hostile toward Assyria. In order to crush this rebellion, Ashurnasirpal marched his army to the Euphrates, where he had to ferry the troops using an unconventional strategy, namely using inflated goat skins. The Assyrian king crushed the rebelling forces, destroyed their cities, and deported their population. The Aramean state of Bit Adini supported this anti-Assyrian rebellion and thus had to answer for it. Ashurnasirpal launched yet another campaign, this time in the territories of Bit Adini, probably the very next year (the exact date is unknown). He destroyed the fortress city of Kaprabu, massacring and enslaving its population. Ashurnasirpal did not strive to conquer Bit Adini; he just wanted to pacify the region. However, he did receive a significant tribute from its ruler, Ahuni. It seemed that Ahuni accepted the Assyrian victory, and he remained at peace with them for the time being. But later, during the reign of Ashurnasirpal's son Shalmaneser III, he would lead another uprising in this region and witness his state being run into the ground.

After pacifying these Aramean lands, Ashurnasirpal was ready to begin his campaign in Syria. His first objective was Carchemish, the capital city of the Neo-Hittites. Its ruler was a man named Sangara, who, upon the arrival of the Assyrian army, surrendered the city without resistance. Carchemish was, during this period, one of the most prosperous Hittite cities, and its capture brought enormous riches to the Assyrian king. The city paid tribute to Ashurnasirpal, giving him 20 talents of silver, 100 talents of bronze, 250 talents of iron, as well as furniture, thrones, elephant tusks, a couch and a chariot made completely out of gold, 200 girls, and the entire army of the city, which included infantry, chariotry, and cavalry. With this payment, Sangara ensured that the Assyrian army would not destroy the city. After the surrender of Carchemish, Ashurnasirpal declared that all the kings of this region now bowed to him, which might indicate that they were intimidated by the fall of Carchemish and, as a result, surrendered. They probably paid handsome tributes to Ashurnasirpal and ensured even more troops for his expeditions deeper into Syria. To make sure newly conquered lands would stay submissive to his rule, Ashurnasirpal took seventy hostages from them. These hostages had to accompany him on his march toward the Mediterranean.

Ashurnasirpal then began conquering Syria's coastal states, which took him to the northernmost parts of the Neo-Hittite kingdoms. Here, he conquered Patin, a Luwian Neo-Hittite state that the Assyrians called Unqi. Control of Patin ensured Ashurnasirpal had dominion over the entire Levantine coast.

Luash was the first state in Syria that gathered an armed resistance against Ashurnasirpal's army. However, they were no match for the Assyrian army, which destroyed its cities and massacred its people. The defending forces were impaled in front of the ruins of the cities to serve as a warning to any other state that contemplated resistance against the Neo-Assyrian Empire. News of Luash's fate traveled well before Ashurnasirpal while he marched to Mount Lebanon. The rulers of the Phoenician cities of this region complied with Assyrian demands in order to avoid the destruction of their lands. Upon reaching the Mediterranean, Ashurnasirpal declared his victory over the Levantine coast. Many of the riches gathered during this Syrian campaign served as building materials for the construction of Ashurnasirpal's new capital of Kalhu, better known as Nimrud. Conquering the Syrian lands, Ashurnasirpal opened trade routes toward the west. Western states had to pay Assyria a tribute to ensure their freedom. As long as they kept paying, Ashurnasirpal promised he wouldn't lead military campaigns into their lands.

Ashurnasirpal also conquered a number of Phoenician/Canaanite cities, but he chose not to destroy them. Instead, he collected a yearly tribute, which he used to equip his army as well as to invest in the further development of the Assyrian capital. The only failure was the siege of Tyre, but this Phoenician city decided to pay tribute to Assyria to ensure no further attacks on its walls. Tyre was the main trade route to Rhodes and Miletus, and due to its tribute, it became a significant source of raw materials for the Assyrian Empire.

Shalmaneser III, the son of Ashurnasirpal II, ruled the Neo-Assyrian Empire between 859 and 824. He continued his father's practice of yearly military expeditions during his long reign. He warred against the eastern tribes, Babylonia, the nations of Mesopotamia and Syria, and the Anatolian kingdom of Kizzuwadna and Urartu. He also subdued the kingdoms of Hamath and Aram Damascus. Thirty-four of Shalmaneser's military campaigns were recorded, with nineteen taking place across the Euphrates in the Hittite regions. There, he encountered a much more serious resistance than his father because the western states had formed a coalition. Their common enemy, the Assyrian Empire, had brought together the Neo-Hittite kingdoms and their rulers. Upon Shalmaneser's entrance in Syria, he received tribute from Hattusili, the king of Kummuh, and Muwatalli, king of Gurgum; however, his next target proved to be more resilient. In the Aramean kingdom of Sam'al, he encountered the allied forces of Bit Adini, Carchemish, Sam'al, and Patin. Individually, none of these kingdoms stood a chance against the might of the Assyrian army, but together, they proved to be a bigger challenge. Assyrian records tell the story of a great victory Shalmaneser achieved, but reality might be different. He was victorious against the allied kingdoms, but he did not destroy their lands or slaughter their armies. Shortly after, he once again had to encounter the same allied forces on the battlefield. Shalmaneser defeated them a second time, and in tribute to himself, he erected a great statue inscribed with the records of his victory. But this victory seemed to have achieved little, for yet another anti-Assyrian alliance was called together by King Suppiluliuma of Patin. The kingdoms of Adanawa, Hilakku, Yasbuq, and Yahan answered Suppiluliuma's call and gathered their forces near the city of Alimush. Despite the size of the newly formed alliance forces, they were no match for the well-trained and organized army of the

Assyrian Empire. Shalmaneser was victorious yet again, and he gained complete control of the Syrian states.

By taking northern Syria, Shalmaneser opened the way to conquer the richer states and cities to the south. He launched a new campaign into the valley of Orontes, where he attacked Hamath, which was ruled by King Irhuleni, and completely destroyed the northern cities of Adennu, Parga, and Argana. The central and southern parts of Irhuleni's kingdom were still intact, and the king chose to call for a new alliance against Assyria rather than to succumb under its rule. This is where Shalmaneser encountered a second coalition, but this one included eleven states. Shalmaneser's scribe recorded between 50,000 and 60,000 infantry units, 4,000 chariots, 2,000 cavalry units, and 1,000 camels belonging to the enemy forces, but these numbers might be exaggerated due to propaganda. However, even if the armies are scaled down to their more probable numbers, the forces Shalmaneser encountered were considerable. The main leaders of the allied forces were King Irhuleni of Hamath and King Hadadezer of Damascus.

The Assyrian army confronted the allied forces in the city of Qarqar in 853. The Battle of Qarqar is a point in history where the Arabs are, for the first time, mentioned in scripts. Details of the battle are unknown, but Shalmaneser boasts how he defeated his enemies and fought them from the city of Qarqar to the city of Gilzau. Furthermore, he proclaims that he slaughtered 14,000 troops and also speaks of making a bridge over Orontes with the bodies of enemy soldiers.

Shalmaneser's victory proved that numbers alone were not enough to defeat the Assyrian army. The diversity of allied forces may have, in fact, hindered the coalition as they were not disciplined or accustomed to fighting together. However, all the leaders of the alliance survived with the chance to fight another day, because their coalition would reform once again in the future and defy Shalmaneser one more time.

In just two campaigns, led in 851 and 850, Shalmaneser conquered parts of Babylonia. This conquest started due to Babylonia being divided between two brothers, Marduk-zakir-shumi I and Marduk-bel-usati. The elder brother, Marduk-zakir-shumi, asked Shalmaneser for help in subduing his brother. He risked unleashing the Assyrian hordes in his own lands in hopes he would subdue his rebellious brother, so he must have been in great need for help since he asked not just for some troops but for the whole Assyrian army and King Shalmaneser himself as their leader. Marduk-bel-usati stood no chance against the Assyrians, and his rebellion ended. But it took two campaigns to finish what was started with the invitation of the Babylonian king. The city of Gannanate, where Marduk-bel-usati himself was hiding, resisted the first attack. However, in the second year of the Babylonian campaign, Shalmaneser managed to conquer Gannanate, plundering its treasures and massacring its population. Marduk-bel-usati escaped the city and hid on the mountain Arman, but there, his luck ran out, and he was caught and killed.

After finishing the campaigns in Babylonia, Shalmaneser once again turned his sights to the west, where an uprising against Assyria was brewing and where he would have to face the coalition of eleven states for the second time. In 848, Shalmaneser marched to meet his enemies in the land of Hamath. He claimed he conquered ninety cities during his march to finally confront the combined forces of the Syrian-Palestinian lands. The alliance suffered a heavy defeat, but several years later, they regrouped and challenged the Assyrian king once again.

Three years later, in 845, Shalmaneser returned to put an end to the Syrian-Palestinian coalition. However, the leader of the allied forces, King Hadadezer, died at an unknown date between 845 and 841, and so, the coalition fell apart, leaving Aram-Damascus to fight Assyria alone. In 841, Shalmaneser claimed victory over Aram-Damascus, but Hazael, the new king, fled to the city of Damascus, where the Assyrian army blockaded him. Even three years later, Shalmaneser could not take Damascus, even though he destroyed its surroundings, blocked trade routes, and destroyed its fields and orchards. However, Israel and a number of Phoenician cities sent tribute to Shalmaneser, accepting his rule.

In 839, Shalmaneser decided to attack the lands of Adanawa in southeastern Anatolia. The motive to attack here can be found in the invitation the king of Sam'al, Kilamuwa, sent to Shalmaneser, who wanted the Assyrian king to come and help him take the lands of the Danunians (Adanawa). In the first campaign in the Adanawa lands, Shalmaneser claimed he conquered three fortified cities called Lusanda, Abarnanu, and Kisuatnu. It took three more military expeditions to finally subdue Adanawa in 833. However, previously in 836, Shalmaneser conquered the territory of Tabal, which, together with Adanawa, marked the end of the Assyrian expansion under the rule of King Shalmaneser III. Any other military campaign led by him was purely against uprisings and rebellions in his own lands against his son Assur-danin-pal.

The eldest son would almost destroy the Assyrian Empire, as 27 cities joined Assur-danin-pal. But the rebellion wasn't against the king himself but rather because some of the governors took too much power. This rebellion was quashed by Shalmaneser's younger son and successor, Shamshi-Adad V, who would rule from 824 to 811 BCE.

The reign of Shamshi-Adad V was marked by his campaigns against Mesopotamia. In 814, he launched several campaigns into Babylonian territory, with the main battle taking place at the city of Dur-Papsukkal. This city was located in the Diyala region (part of today's Iraq) in eastern Babylonia. Opposing Shamshi-Adad was the son of Marduk-zakir-shumi I, Marduk-balassu-iqbi. The Assyrians claimed victory in this battle, but it seems that the result was somewhat inconclusive because Shamshi-Adad launched another campaign against Babylonia in 813, this time with the main battle taking place near Der, another city in the same region. Marduk-balassu-iqbi was captured and taken as a prisoner to Assyria. In the next year, the Assyrians had to return to Babylonia and confront their new king, Baba-aha-iddina, who, like his predecessor, was taken prisoner to Assyria as well. Babylonia was left in chaos and anarchy for the next sixty years until 747 when King Nabonassar took control.

Shamshi-Adad's son, Adad-nirari III, ruled between 810 and 783. He turned his attention toward the west, across the Euphrates, where their neighbors were enjoying a brief moment of peace. Adad-nirari started his campaigns to the west in 805, where he confronted a coalition of states, just like his grandfather had. Eight kings formed an alliance, which was led by Attar-shumki, the king of the Aramean Kingdom of Arpad (Bit Agusi). Adad-nirari was victorious over this coalition, but he did not manage to break up the alliance. For the next ten years of his rule, this alliance would continue to defy him. During his reign, though, he managed to invade the Levant and conquer the Arameans, Phoenicians, Philistines, Israelites, and Neo-Hittites there. He even conquered Damascus, but he left the royal family of Ben-Hadad III to rule it. Instead, Adad-nirari satisfied himself with taking a yearly tribute from him. He continued his conquests in Iran, where he subjugated the Persians, Medes, and Mannaeans, and he continued his conquest all the way to the Caspian Sea. Adad-nirari's final military expeditions were to the southern Mesopotamian region, where he conquered the Chaldean and Sutu tribes and imposed a vassal status on their states. However, his premature death in 783 was the beginning of a stagnation period for the Neo-Assyrian Empire when it came to their expansion policy.

An interesting fact of Adad-nirari's campaign to the west was the presence of his mother, Sammuramat, who followed her son on military expeditions and who claimed some military victories in her own name. She is a persona that is mentioned in history but also in the myths that are part of the classical tradition. In various Assyrian inscriptions, she is mentioned often as a "palace woman" of King Shamshi-Adad V and the daughter-in-law of the great Shalmaneser III. In legends, she is known as Semiramis, and she shows up in

Greek sources as well as in various texts from Near Eastern states. The victory of Bactria was attributed to her, but she was also known for building the walls of Babylon and some other prominent monuments around the country. Armenian sources mention her as a conqueror of Urartu. Whether the sources are accurate or just an exaggeration of her persona is unknown. However, the king's mother following her son on military expeditions must have been an unusual sight. She was undoubtedly a person of unprecedented importance in the Assyrian Empire, as she is mentioned in various important scripts and documents, and she also had a royal stele of her own.

The period of stagnation of the Neo-Assyrian Empire lasted from 783 to 745. It is commonly believed that the successor to Adad-nirari III, Shalmaneser IV, was a weak ruler, and any military conquests during the time of his rule were accredited to his general, Shamshi-ilu.

In 772, Ashur-dan III took the throne, but he also proved to be a weak ruler. He had to deal with rebellions in some of his cities, including Ashur, Arrapkha, and Guzana. He tried to gain more Babylonian and Syrian territory, but he failed in his military campaigns. Shortly following his footsteps was yet another weak king, Ashur-nirari V, and his reign was marked by internal state turmoil and rebellions.

Finally, in 744, Tiglath-Pileser III ascended to the throne and brought reassurance to Assyria. It is common belief that he was a member of the same dynasty, but Tiglath-Pileser supported the uprising against Ashur-nirari V. Some historians claim he was even his son, but there is no evidence to support this claim. Some historians see Tiglath-Pileser as a usurper who took advantage of the uprisings against the previous king in order to claim the crown for himself. Whatever his path to the throne was, he became king at just the right time. The internal struggles of the Neo-Assyrian Empire were so turbulent that they could have crushed the empire had it not been for Tiglath-Pileser.

During the stagnant period in Assyria, the Kingdom of Urartu took some of the northern Mesopotamian territories and conquered some former Assyrian tributaries. However, Tiglath-Pileser didn't wait, and in the second year of reign, he launched a military expedition to regain the lost territories. He started with the land of Namri, which was located in the upper Diyala River Valley. The Assyrian army was merciless in subjugating these lands, and other states east of the Euphrates were quick to submit to the new Assyrian king. In 743, Tiglath-Pileser turned westward and tried to regain control of kingdoms across the Euphrates, but he had to face a combined force of the Kingdoms of Arpad and Urartu. This alliance was led by Sarduri II of Urartu, but the Neo-Hittite king of Malataya joined, as well as Gurgum and Kummuh. Tiglath-Pileser reports his victory in the battle fought in Kummuh's territory. Sarduri was brutally defeated and had to retreat back to his own lands in Urartu. The kings of Malataya, Gurgum, and Kummuh accepted their defeat and submitted themselves to the Assyrian king. They were all pardoned and became tributaries to the Assyrian Empire.

Arpad still had to be dealt with, and this state was of particular interest to Tiglath-Pileser as it was Urartu's strongest ally. However, its capital city resisted the Assyrian siege for three years until it finally fell. There are no detailed records of the siege itself, just a mention of the city's fall in the Eponym Chronicles. An Assyrian governor was installed in this region, making Arpad an Assyrian province. This event paved the path for the provincialization process Tiglath-Pileser undertook regarding western vassal states. In 739, his attention was drawn toward the east, where the Kingdom of Ulluba was planning an invasion on Assyrian territory and had the support of neighboring Urartu. However, Tiglath-Pileser reacted immediately and was successful in his campaign against Ulluba, which was then converted into a province of the Assyrian Empire.

The process of turning former tributary states into Assyrian provinces continued, as this was the way Tiglath-Pileser III consolidated his power over the conquered territories. To further secure his dominion over these regions, Tiglath-Pileser relocated the local populations into other regions of the empire and then replaced their numbers with people from other regions. Another purpose for these relocations was to break any possible alliances between former neighbors and to secure the new borders of the Assyrian Empire. At this time, the Assyrian army became a professional one, with each province sending a military contingent. The changes the Assyrians went through with Tiglath-Pileser as its king are often referred to as the "Second Assyrian Empire."

The first Neo-Hittite kingdom that became an Assyrian province and underwent the process of population relocation was Patin in 738, which was called Kullani. The rest soon followed. In the same year, Tiglath-Pileser decided to invade Israel and impose a large tribute on King Menahem. He also did the same to Azariah, the king of Judah, and Azriyau, the king of Sam'al. Furthermore, in 732, Tiglath-Pileser finally conquered Damascus, as it had been lost since the time of Adad-Nirari III due to rebellions, and began the process of turning it into a province. A few years later, in 727, Tiglath-Pileser III died, but not before he crowned himself as the new king of Babylonia, calling himself King Pulu.

Tiglath-Pileser III was succeeded by Shalmaneser V, who ruled very briefly from 727 to 722. During his short reign, he attacked Samaria (Israel) and took its capital city, also named Samaria, but only after three years of siege. King Hoshea of Israel was corresponding with the Egyptian pharaoh, Osorkon IV, who sent an army to help Israel fight Assyria. Egypt wanted a foothold in the land of Samaria, but Shalmaneser V could not allow the territories of his vassal kingdom to be taken. Shalmaneser V died during an expedition in Israel and was succeeded by his brother and commander of his armies, Sargon II, who ended the campaign in Israel quickly.

Sargon was already a middle-aged man when he took the throne. Some historians speculate that he was the one who disposed of his brother in order to ascend to the throne. Nevertheless, the beginning of his reign was marked with widespread rebellions. In Babylonia,

Marduk-apla-iddina II proclaimed himself king and took the crown in 721, claiming Babylonia's independence from Assyrian rule. Sargon met Marduk-apla-iddina in battle near the city of Der in 720, where the Assyrian army was pushed back, allowing Babylonia to retrieve its territories in the south. Sargon did not give up on Babylonia, as he fought Marduk-apla-iddina many more times, and each time, Sargon was victorious. In 710, Marduk-apla-iddina abandoned his position as the king of Babylonia as he had to flee for his life. Babylonia surrendered and, once again, became a part of the Assyrian Empire in 709. Marduk-apla-iddina continued his rebellion against Assyria, though, and led military operations against them. This continued until the rule of Sargon's son, Sennacherib, who finally defeated Marduk-apla-iddina in 703.

In 718, Sargon led a campaign in Tabal, a Neo-Hittite kingdom in south-central Anatolia. He had to secure the entire territory of Tabal against the Phrygians in the northwestern territories, who often organized military incursions that endangered Assyrian borders. In order to achieve this, Sargon created one united kingdom of southern Anatolia named Bit-Burutash, with the Assyrian ruler Ambaris as its king.

Right after his campaign in Tabal, Sargon II received the news that the king of Carchemish, Pisiri, was secretly communicating with Mita, the king of the Mushki, which was an act of treason since it broke the treaty Carchemish had with Assyria. Sargon could not risk losing the strategically positioned city of Carchemish, as it would damage Assyrian authority in the western regions. Without even allowing Pisiri to explain his actions, Sargon attacked his kingdom, plundered it, and took its king and his whole family back to Assyria. In 717, Carchemish became an Assyrian province and ceased to exist as an independent kingdom.

In 714, Sargon decided to make a preemptive strike against the Urartian kingdom. A possible motivation for this was Urartu's weakness after numerous incursions by the Cimmerians, a nomadic tribe of the steppes. This was Sargon's eighth military campaign, and it was against King Rusa I, the ruler of Urartu. The campaign was well documented by Sargon himself in his letter to the god Ashur. He wrote about one of his armies that had to cut a forest and disassemble chariots and carry them in order to traverse the impassable terrain toward Urartu. He also mentioned his crushing victory over Rusa's army, making the king of Urartu flee for his life. Urartu was torn apart by the Assyrian military expedition, on top of the existing Cimmerian incursions, and as a result, King Rusa committed suicide after these events.

It is interesting that during the campaigns in 713, Sargon himself did not lead the armies. Instead, he stayed in his capital, and it is unknown why. It is speculated that he acted this way due to his advancing age. His army, however, was successful in taking Cilicia and Karalla, and they successfully completed a campaign in Tabal, while Persia and Mede offered tribute to avoid aggression.

In 711, Sargon had to deal with various unrests in his western provinces, mainly in the state of Gurgum, where King Tarhulara, who was loyal to Assyria, was assassinated by his son, the usurper Muwatalli III. Muwatalli proclaimed Gurgum's independence and probably had secret dealings with the Urartu kingdom, as well as with Phrygia. Sargon responded by aggressively removing Muwatalli from Gurgum's throne, annexing his kingdom and turning it into an Assyrian province, which would hold that status until the fall of the Neo-Assyrian Empire.

During Sargon's rule, the Assyrian Empire was at its highest. Even the Greek kings of Cyprus accepted his sovereignty. Phrygia and its king, Midas, submitted to Assyria in 708, and Kummuh became another Assyrian province as well. Sargon died in 705 while on an expedition to pacify Tabal, which had rebelled under the leadership of Gurdi the Kulummaean.

Sargon II was succeeded by his son Sennacherib, who ruled somewhere between 705 and 681 BCE. There are actually three proposed dates (705, 704, and 703) of his succession, which might imply that his coming to the throne wasn't without some turbulence. His name also indicates he was not Sargon's firstborn son. Sennacherib decided to move the Assyrian capital from Dur-Sharrukin to Nineveh. During the first years of his rule, Sennacherib encountered a problematic rebellion that required his full attention: Cilicia attempted to gain independence with the help of the Greeks. Sennacherib defeated Cilicia's rebels and their Greek allies.

In 701, Sennacherib had to turn toward Babylonia, where his first military campaign started. Marduk-apla-iddina II took the crown of Babylonia yet again, proclaiming himself as king, but his rebellion was short-lived. He was defeated, and once more, he had to run. This time he found sanctuary with his ally, Elam. Strangely enough, even though the city of Babylon was plundered, its population was not harmed. Evidently, Sennacherib either wasn't as bloodthirsty as his predecessors or he saw some possible gain in leaving the citizens alone. On the throne of Babylonia, he placed an Assyrian puppet king called Bel-ibni, and Babylonia remained at peace for some time.

However, Marduk-apla-iddina did not give up on his rebellion against Assyria. Soon after, he allied himself with Egypt. This alliance led to disaster for some of the Canaanite cities that were conquered, among them being Byblos, Ashdod, Ammon, and Edom. They all paid tribute to Sennacherib without further resistance. Egypt was defeated, and then the Assyrian king turned toward Jerusalem. He besieged the city but never captured it. Biblical sources mention an intervention from God's angels who smote 180,000 Assyrian soldiers; however, reality wasn't nearly as dramatic nor devastating. Sennacherib's scribe mentions a tribute being paid by the Kingdom of Judah, which satisfied Sennacherib, who decided to leave the city's gates.

Marduk-apla-iddina again tried to incite a rebellion against Assyrian rule, this time backed with his allies from Elam. In 694, Sennacherib destroyed the Elamite base in the Persian Gulf with the help of the Phoenician fleet, but while he was doing this, the Elamites managed to capture his eldest son, Ashur-nadin-shumi. They also placed Nergal-ushezib, the son of Marduk-apla-iddina II, on the Babylonian throne. Babylon fell under Assyrian rule in 689 but not after a few more attempts at rebellion. Unfortunately, it took a great amount of destruction and devastation for Sennacherib to finally put an end to the Babylonian problem.

Very little is known about his rule in the following years, and Sennacherib was assassinated in 681, most likely by one of his sons. He was succeeded by Esarhaddon, who describes the unrest that followed Sennacherib's death and how he took the throne while his brothers were fighting over it. He doesn't mention a possible murderer, but this may be because he tried to avoid further dynastic unrest. Other sources, like the Babylonian Chronicles, various biblical documents, and later Assyrian documents, imply that Sennacherib was murdered by one of his sons.

Esarhaddon ruled from 681 until 669 BCE and was the youngest son of Sennacherib. His first military excursions were against the Aramean tribes in southern Mesopotamia. During the first years of his rule, he had to reinforce the borders of his empire, as its provinces were under attack by the Cimmerians from the shores of the Black Sea, as well as by the Scythians who crossed the Taurus Mountains, coming from the southern steppes of today's Russia.

In 677, the king of Sidon, Abdi-Milkutti, rose against Assyria, but he was quickly defeated and beheaded. The capital city of Sidon was completely destroyed but was rebuilt as Kar-Ashur-aha-iddina. Esarhaddon continued the tradition of repopulating newly conquered areas with people from other parts of his empire in order to secure his dominance in the region.

The Scythians proved to be a nuisance to Assyrian rule. In 676, Esarhaddon conquered the cities of Sissu and Kundu in the Taurus Mountains before bringing King Ishpakia of the Scythians to heel. After the fall of Phrygia, Esarhaddon gave his own daughter to be wed to the Scythian prince, Partatua of Sakasene. This act was done in order to improve relations between the Assyrian Empire and the Scythian nomads, as well as to assure their loyalty.

The most important military campaign during Esarhaddon's rule was against Egypt and Pharaoh Taharqa of the Nubian dynasty. Esarhaddon left parts of his army to deal with a rebellion in Tyre, and with the remaining army, he took Egyptian lands. In the summer of 671, Esarhaddon reached Memphis, and with the help of some of the Egyptian princes, he captured it, forcing Taharqa to flee back into Nubia. Memphis was raided and sacked, its citizens were slaughtered, and their heads were gathered in piles in order to warn the Egyptians against rebellion. However, as soon as Esarhaddon left, Egypt rebelled. It was Esarhaddon's son, Ashurbanipal, who would continue to fight Egypt. It is believed that Esarhaddon died due to an illness. There are texts written by him that talk about his weak constitution during his final years. But there is also a possibility of him abdicating in favor of his son in 668 and that he died a year later.

Ashurbanipal succeeded his father and ruled between 668 and 627. He continued his father's efforts in Egypt but was also distracted from time to time by insurgents from the Medes in the east and the Cimmerians and Scythians in the northern territories of the Assyrian Empire. Ashurbanipal is considered the last strong ruler of the Neo-Assyrian Empire; after his death, the empire began its continuous decline. He was also a popular king amongst his subjects but was known to be very cruel and bloodthirsty toward his enemies.

Ashurbanipal didn't personally lead his first military campaign in Egypt. He chose to stay in his capital city Nineveh, but the army he sent managed to defeat Pharaoh Taharqa's army near Memphis. However, they failed to capture or kill Taharqa, and he fled to Upper Egypt. Soon after, in 664, he died, and his nephew, Tantamani, took his place and invaded the Assyrians in Egypt, killing all the nobility that remained loyal to the Assyrian Empire. As a result, Ashurbanipal sent an army to Egypt once again, and this time, he also employed a number of Carian mercenaries from western

Anatolia. Ashurbanipal defeated Tantamani, invading Egypt all the way to Thebes, which he sacked. Eventually, Egypt gained its independence under Pharaoh Psamtik I, who remained on friendly terms with Assyria. It is not known how Psamtik managed to do this, but from that point onward, Egypt was free of Assyrian rule.

During the rule of Ashurbanipal, Assyria was one of the largest empires known to the civilized world. It stretched from the Caucasus in the north to North Africa in the south, and from Cyprus in the west to central Iran in the east. Ashurbanipal's empire was vast, and he decided to start a dual monarchy by installing his own brother, Shamash-shum-ukin, as a vassal ruler in Mesopotamia. At first, Shamash-shum-ukin accepted vassalage under his brother, but soon after, he rebelled and became a Babylonian nationalist. He allied himself with other people who were known for their anti-Assyrian policy. Among them were the Suteans, Chaldeans, Arameans, Persians, Arabs, and the divided kingdom of Elam. Shamash-shum-ukin sent a letter to his brother, declaring he was the ruler and that Ashurbanipal was to become his subject and the governor of Nineveh. Ashurbanipal delayed his attack against his brother due to various bad omens, but when he finally launched an attack, he was victorious. The city of Babylon was besieged for two years until Shamash-shum-ukin committed suicide, as the defeat of the city was imminent. After this, the city surrendered to the Assyrian forces. Ashurbanipal decided not to destroy the city, but he did massacre all of the rebels and their allies. Babylon kept its semi-autonomous status and even formalized it.

Assyria was peaceful during the last years of Ashurbanipal's reign. But overexpansion took its toll on the empire, and it started to decline. Ashurbanipal managed to hold his grasp over the whole empire while he lived. It was after his death that Assyria was torn apart by its constant internal struggles.

Ashurbanipal was succeeded by his son Ashur-etil-ilani, whose reign was very brief, lasting from 631 until 627 BCE. Immediately after taking the throne, he faced civil wars and rebellions throughout the whole empire. These civil wars were just the start of the rapid decline of the empire. Brothers fought for the throne, dividing the Assyrian citizens in who they supported. Sinsharishkun, another son of Ashurbanipal, seized the throne for himself somewhere around 622. Little is known about the last kings of the Neo-Assyrian Empire, as this period lacks sources. Assyria's colonies, provinces, and vassal states took the opportunity brought by the internal upheaval and broke off, claiming their independence. Amongst them were Chaldeans, Babylonians, Medes, Scythians, Sagartians, and Cimmerians. The Assyrian king was in no position to send any armies in order to reclaim those territories because he had to fight a civil war that was tearing the empire apart.

Of all the states that claimed independence, Babylonia posed the most serious threat, and a long war in the heart of this kingdom started. The rebelling citizens of Babylonia gathered under the rule of Nabopolassar, a leader of the Chaldean tribe that resided in southeastern Mesopotamia. He was Babylonia's new king, and he played a key role in the fall of the Neo-Assyrian Empire. Nabopolassar took Babylon as his capital, proclaimed himself king, and ruled Babylonia from 626 to 605. He was the founder of the Neo-Babylonian Empire.

Sinsharishkun did not want to allow Babylonia to regain its freedom. Instead, he gathered his armies and initiated a new military campaign. However, in the heart of Assyria, another rebellion started, and he had to send some of his forces back home. These troops, instead of defeating the rebels, chose to join them, and a new usurper began to threaten Sinsharishkun's throne. There are no records detailing who the usurper was and how the rebellion started as all the sources were probably destroyed during the civil war in Assyria's capital of Nineveh. Sinsharishkun managed to fight off the rebel forces and take the throne again, but he lost the opportunity to solve the Babylonian problem.

Nabopolassar had the time he needed to take Babylonia under his rule and secure his power. In 619, he captured Nippur, thus becoming the ruler of Babylonia. Then he tried to invade the Assyrian territories, but he was defeated and forced back to Babylon. For the next four years, Nabopolassar had to defend his throne from the Assyrian army that was trying to unseat him.

In 616, Nabopolassar had to form an alliance with the Medes in order to fight Assyria, who had joined forces with Egypt. Nabopolassar's alliance was joined by the Scythians and Cimmerians, as well as with the Iranians, Sagartians, and Persians, whose lands he freed from Assyrian rule during the civil war. Now he had an army powerful enough to confront the Assyrian forces. In the following years, the Assyrian cities of Assur, Kalhu, Arbela, and Gasur, among others, were taken. Nineveh itself was besieged for over three months before it fell. This is probably where Sinsharishkun died, but the information about him is missing as the Babylonian Chronicles describing the siege of Nineveh have been damaged. Even though Assyria lost so many cities, it still endured with Harran being its new capital.

Assyria's last king was Ashur-Uballit II (ruled 612 to 608). He was a general in the Assyrian army, and it is speculated that he was the brother of Sinsharishkun, as he was a member of the royal family. He somehow managed to escape the siege of Nineveh, and with the help of the Egyptian army, he defended Harran. He resisted Babylon and its allies for some time, but in 610, the Egyptian armies were depleted, and he had to retreat home. In 609, the Babylonians, Medes, and Scythians sacked Harran. Ashur-Uballit II escaped the city and asked Egypt for help once more. Pharaoh Necho II joined him, and Ashur-Uballit marched his forces toward Assyria. However, the way was blocked by Josiah of Judah and his forces, who had allied themselves with Babylonia. The Egyptian armies had no problem defeating Babylonia, but they arrived to assist Ashur-Uballit in a weakened state. Nevertheless, the joined forces of Assyria and Egypt besieged Harran in 609, but they failed since their armies had been defeated.

Pharaoh Necho II retreated to northern Syria, and it is not known what happened to Ashur-Uballit as this is the last year where his name is mentioned. He disappeared from history, losing the Assyrian Empire forever.

Chapter 5 – The Cimmerians

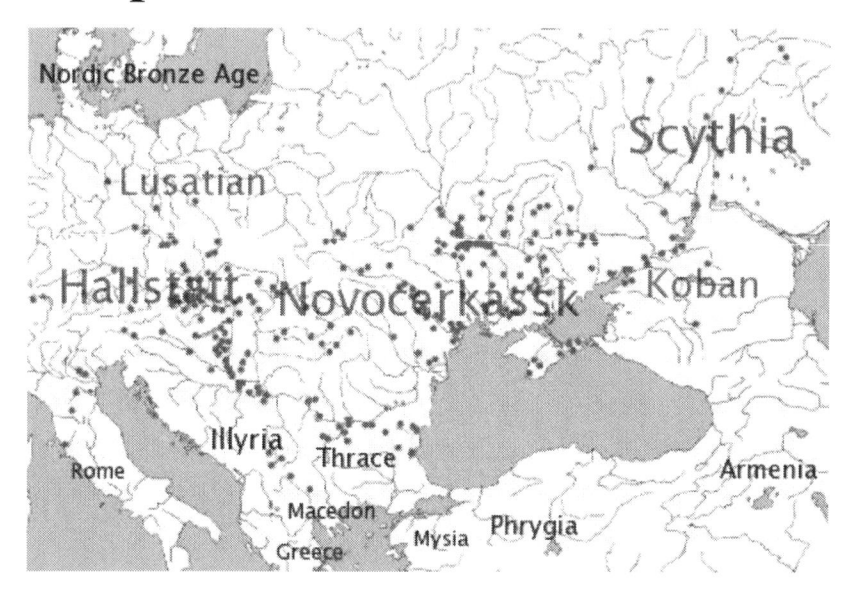

Distribution of "Thraco-Cimmerian" finds

The Cimmerians are a group of people shrouded in mystery. Their existence is known through various sources of Assyrian, Scythian, and Greek origin, but their homeland is never mentioned. Their ethnicity and geographical affiliations are unknown as well. There is no archeological evidence of any kind that would allow historians to say for sure it is of Cimmerian origin. This is why terms like the

"Cimmerian problem," "Cimmerian enigma," or "Cimmerian mystery" are commonly used.

Herodotus, the famous Greek historian, mentions the Cimmerians and claims their origin was from north of the Black sea, in the area of Crimea. Furthermore, he wrote that the Cimmerians were driven out of their lands by hordes of Scythians during the 7th century BCE. The Cimmerians are generally accepted to be of Scythian culture, but they share no ethnic bonds with them. Historians usually relate them to the Iranians or Thracians that had to migrate due to pressure from the Scythian expansion during the 9th century. Herodotus' thoughts on the Cimmerians were accepted as true until the 19th century when new archeological discoveries were made, namely the Assyrian clay tablets dating from approximately 714 BCE. These tablets, from the time of King Sargon II, mention the Cimmerians and specifically their nation of Gamir. This means that by the 8th century, the Cimmerians were settled not far away from Urartu. This places their homeland to the south instead of the north, which was how it was previously believed. The Assyrian tablets may be more accurate in giving information about the Cimmerians; after all, they are several centuries older. But the teachings of Herodotus are not so easily dismissed. Instead, there is a widespread opinion that the newly discovered Assyrian tablets confirm the Cimmerian presence south of the Caucasus, where they wandered during their migration to Asia Minor.

Herodotus placed the Cimmerian migration due to the Scythian attacks during the 7th century, but the Assyrian texts proved it to be even earlier. The assumption is that the migration the Cimmerians undertook happened somewhere during the 8th century and possibly even the 9th century BCE. Because of what the Assyrian sources had to tell, some historians proposed the Cimmerian homeland not to be near the Bosporus in northwestern Turkey or the Pontic Steppe in today's Ukraine but somewhere to the east of Urartu. This is an area that they inhabited during Sargon II's rule and in the century that followed. There was never any archeological evidence found in the area of the Pontic steppe that would even remotely shed light on the Cimmerians' presence in those areas. Even archeological findings in the area of the Black Sea that were attributed to the Cimmerians might be from some other Late Bronze Age or Early Iron age cultures. Historians also never found more evidence for the Cimmerians actually being in the areas of the Bosporus besides their mention in Greek traditions. But this might also be because the Greeks met some other culture that was similar to that of the Cimmerians. The answer to the question where do the Cimmerians come from is based on shaky ground, as there is no evidence that will, for sure, give us a clue where to look.

The land of Gamir was first mentioned in a letter sent to King Sargon II of the Neo-Assyrian Empire. In this letter, the informants from the empire's border with Urartu sent a report to the king describing how Gamir suffered at the hand of Rusa I, the king of Urartu. This letter even contained the specific location of Gamir, saying that the land of Guriania separates Gamir from Urartu. But some linguistic problems are encountered in later studies. Historians often think of Gamir as a dialectic version of Kamir, which is in Cappadocia (modern-day central Turkey), and that would put this kingdom to the west of Urartu. This position would then identify today's Gurunt as the land of Guriania, which would have separated Urartu from Gamir. But later sources, from the time of King Esarhaddon, mention Gamir in the same context as the Mannaeans, Medes, and Umman-Manda, who operated in the northeast of Mesopotamia, which would place Gamir to the east of Urartu.

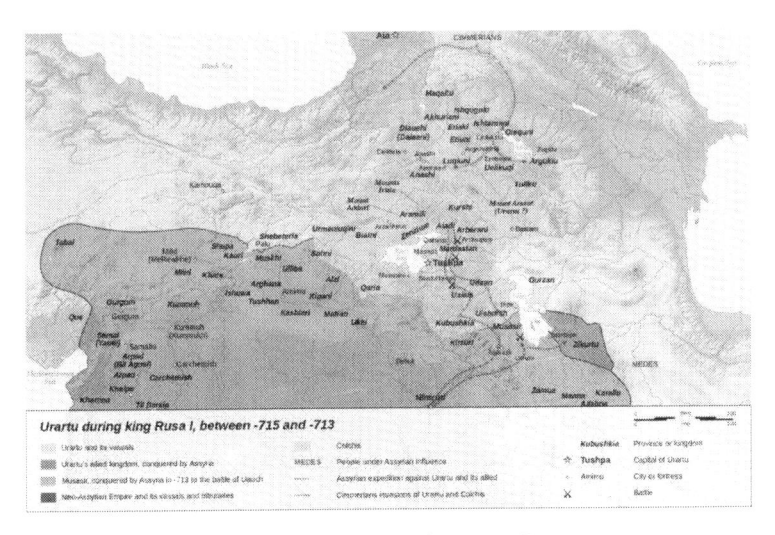

Map of Urartu between 715 and 713 BCE

From the letter to Sargon II, historians were made aware of a battle taking place in Gamir. Apparently, Urartu was at war with the Cimmerians inhabiting these lands at that time. The reason for the war is still unknown, but the letter specifically describes King Rusa I of Urartu fleeing from Gamir in defeat. Because the letter was dated from being around 714 BCE, most scholars agree that the Battle of Gamir must have happened somewhere around that year, maybe even in 715.

Another Assyrian intelligence report dating from approximately the same time describes the Cimmerian invasion of Urartu, but this time from the territories of Mannea, a land south of Lake Urmia. Some scholars claim that this report also refers to the Battle of Gamir, but the context of the letter is completely different. Instead of Rusa attacking Gamir and losing the battle, the Cimmerians were the aggressors who invaded Urartu. The difference in context leads to the conclusion that this was a second confrontation the Cimmerians had with King Rusa I. Most likely, the Cimmerians joined Sargon II in the war against Urartu, and the combined forces were victorious, driving Rusa to commit suicide.

There are numerous mentions of the Cimmerians in Assyrian documents, but they only describe battles. The Assyrians were a military empire, prone to expansion; therefore, the majority of their surviving documents are battle reports. There are still no accounts that would explain the Cimmerian culture, ethnicity, politics, or economy.

From many Assyrian reports, it is known that Transcaucasia was a base from which the Cimmerians attacked and raided the Assyrian borders or the Assyrian vassal states. However, in 679, the Cimmerians were defeated by the Assyrian army led by King Esarhaddon. This is when the Cimmerian king is mentioned by name for the first time. According to Esarhaddon, the Cimmerian king was named Teushpa, but he also mentions him as the king of the Umman-Manda, which is Akkadian for "the horde from who knows where." This term was used to describe a poorly known tribe of the ancient Near East. The Umman-Manda have been attributed to different peoples the Assyrians fought in their history: Hurrians, Medes, Cimmerians, Elamites, and Scythians. It is thought they came from central Anatolia, but the Akkadian saying pretty much sums up how historians view this culture.

During the same year of 679, a Cimmerian detachment of soldiers was serving in the Assyrian army. At one point, the Cimmerians allied themselves with the Medes, attacking Shubria (a country bordering Lake Van), Parsua, and maybe even Ellipi. Again in 671/70, there are mentions of the Cimmerians serving in the Assyrian army.

Another Cimmerian king mentioned by name was Tugdamme, better known as Dugdammi in classical Greek teachings. He ruled during the mid-seventh century, presumably between 660 and 640. He is known for attacking the Greek cities in coastal Asia Minor. But in 653, he turned his attention toward the Assyrian Empire, which was ruled by King Ashurbanipal at that time. Assyrian reports on this confrontation mention Tugdamme as the king of Saka and Qutium, a nomadic people of the northern, eastern, and western parts of the

Eurasian Steppe. Ashurbanipal also called him "Sar Kissati," which roughly translates to "King of the World." This suggests Tugdamme ruled a vast kingdom. Tugdamme was defeated and killed around 641 or 640 BCE. Assyrian texts mention Marduk (a Mesopotamian deity) killing Tugdamme, which alludes to some other force being responsible for his death, not the Assyrians.

After Tugdamme, Ashurbanipal mentions Tugdamme's son, Sandakhshatra, as being the next king of the Cimmerians. There are some speculations that Sandakhshatra was, in fact, Cyaxares, the king of Media, and that he helped in bringing down the Neo-Assyrian Empire. There is no archeological or historical evidence to support these claims, however.

Ashurbanipal also speaks of a permanent Cimmerian settlement in Anatolia. In 665, the Cimmerians attacked Lydia but were defeated, as Ashurbanipal himself sent help to King Gyges of Lydia. The Cimmerians succeeded in defeating the Lydians, either in 654 or 652, and took over their capital city of Sardis. Gyges died during this battle with the Cimmerians. In 640, under the leadership of King Tugdamme, the Cimmerians attacked the Greek cities of Ionia and Aeolis. There are also mentions of their activity in the regions of Paphlagonia, Bithynia, and Troad. Around the same year, the Cimmerians tried to ally themselves with the Assyrian vassal state of Tabal in order to bring down Assyrian rule, but King Tugdamme fell ill, and it is believed he committed suicide.

The last mention of the Cimmerian people is from the end of the 7th century BCE when the Lydian king, Alyattes, defeated them in eastern Anatolia. From this point onward, sources no longer mention them; however, it is believed they settled in Cappadocia.

Chapter 6 – The Scythians

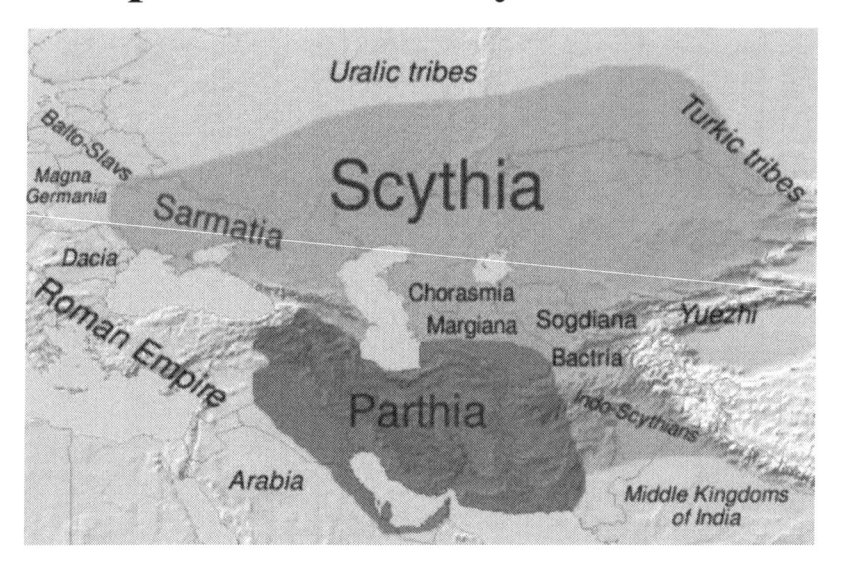

The extent of Eastern Iranian languages in the first century BCE

The word Scythians used to be used in a wider sense, mainly to describe the nomadic peoples of the Eurasian Steppe. What was common for all these people was the nomadic way of life and some similar aspects of culture. This is why today the term "people of Scythian culture" is used to describe various peoples who covered the same territory and shared a similar way of life. But ethnically, these people were different, and in time, historians started making a difference between them.

It is believed that the Scythians are of Iranian origin because their language is a branch of Iranian languages. But they also practiced a form of the Iranian religion. Herodotus noted that the Scythians came from the northern areas of the Black Sea as they pursued the Cimmerian tribes they had driven out of the Pontic Steppe. The Cimmerians crossed the Caucasus Mountains, but the Scythians followed them and entered Anatolia, where they would influence the region from the seventh to third century BCE.

There are two groups of sources that reveal the history of the Scythians. One is in Akkadian cuneiform texts, and the other one is of Greco-Roman origin. The Akkadians reveal only the earliest history of the Scythians, while the Greco-Roman sources cover their whole history. However, Greek sources that refer to early Scythian history, which was the seventh and sixth centuries BCE, are not always reliable. The Greeks often mixed history with common folktales; therefore, reading these sources requires critical analysis. The earliest document that mentions the Scythians is the Assyrian annals of King Esarhaddon, which speaks of a retreat of the Mannaeans after a battle. The Mannaeans at that time had the Scythians for allies, who were under the leadership of Ishpaka. Ishpaka also had the Cimmerians and Medes for allies, and in 678, he planned an invasion of the Assyrian territory. He died in battle against the Assyrian forces, which were led by Esarhaddon, around 675 and was succeeded by Bartatua (or Partatua). Bartatua couldn't keep the alliance whole, and he was defeated by the Assyrians. In order to keep the peace, he agreed to marry Esarhaddon's daughter in 674/6; this act made him an Assyrian vassal. He helped the Assyrians in their conquest of Media somewhere between 653 and 652, and the Assyrians gifted Media to the Scythians as a reward for their help. Bartatua died in 645 BCE. By 620, when the fall of the Neo-Assyrian Empire became inevitable, the Scythians gained more freedom. By taking advantage of the Assyrian situation, they started their own lengthy campaigns.

The Scythian king Madyes (Madius) inherited the throne after Bartatua, and he marched the army to the borders of Egypt. The Scythians plundered the region of Palestine, making the Cimmerians retreat from these territories. According to Herodotus, the next 28 years would be known as the years of Scythian rule over Asia, but Pompeius Trogus, a Roman historian, places the Scythian domination over Asia in a period of only eight years. This is where the influence of Scythian folklore on Herodotus is evident. The reality was that there was no Scythian rule but rather a large number of lengthy and successful raids.

Media finally liberated itself under the rule of King Cyaxares, who killed all the Scythian leaders during a feast at his palace, according to Herodotus. The Scythians stopped raiding the Middle East in the last decade of the seventh century BCE.

During the early sixth century, the Greeks started founding their colonies in the territory ruled by the Scythians on the shores and islands of the Black Sea. The relations between these two people were peaceful at that time, but there is new evidence that suggests the possible destruction of the Greek city Panticapaeum at the hands of the Scythians approximately during the middle of the sixth century.

Probably the most important event in the sixth century in Scythian history was the campaign for the lands of Darius I, a Persian king known for his victorious military expeditions. Before encountering the Scythians, Darius conquered parts of Eastern Europe until he reached the Danube. He invaded European Scythia between 520 and 507. Many historians put the year of this invasion in 513, but it is difficult to pinpoint the year of the invasion based on surviving sources. To cross the Bosporus, Darius I built a bridge out of ships. If Herodotus is to be believed, his army numbered 70,000 men. At the time of the Persian invasion, the Scythians were separated into three kingdoms with three different kings. However, King Idanthyrsus was considered the overlord, while the other two kings, Scopasis and Taxacis, were his subordinates. The Scythians did not receive support from their neighbors in the fight against the Persians, so they decided to implement scorched-earth tactics and moved the civilians with their livestock to the north. Darius chased the Scythians, but they retreated to the east, burning the countryside and blocking the springs and wells, as well as destroying the pastures. The Persian army chased the Scythians in hopes of openly fighting them but found themselves deep into the steppes, where there were no cities to plunder to resupply their army. Darius was frustrated by the Scythian tactics, and he openly challenged King Idanthyrsus to fight or else surrender. Idanthyrsus replied he would not fight Darius until they reached the tombs of the Scythian forefathers. He continued his tactics of retreat, as they had nothing to lose; there were no cities or villages, just open steppes. The Persian army chased the Scythians for a month, and Darius lost a number of his forces due to sickness, fatigue, and constant Scythian skirmishes. Finally, Darius stopped his chase at the banks of the River Volga and turned toward Thrace. However, Darius already conquered so much of the Scythian territory that most of the areas had to submit to Persian rule. Even so, Darius was still considered to have been defeated in this battle.

Even though the Scythians formally lost against the Persians, their endurance made their neighbors see them as invincible. This tradition of thinking of the Scythians as being invincible continued during the classical period, where it found its place mainly in literature.

The Scythians were a nomadic people, which means that they lived in tribes. However, these tribes would form a confederation when it came to the defense of their lands. The Scythian tribes also formed something close to a modern-day institution that would regulate pastures and agricultural lands of these equestrian herdsmen. Animal breeding exceeded the needs of the settled agricultural societies of the Scythians, and they started developing trade with other nearby nomadic peoples.

Herodotus mentions three Scythian tribes that were ruled by three brothers: Lipoxais, Arpoxais, and Colaxais. In folklore, these tribes received divine gifts: a plow, a yoke, an ax, and a bowl (or drinking cup). Traditionally, these three tribes are treated as if they occupied geographically distinct territories, but historians are proposing that the three divine gifts refer to social occupations. This would mean that the plow and yoke are symbols of farmers, the ax is a symbol of warriors, and the bowl or cup represent priests.

When it comes to warfare, almost the entire adult population of the Scythians, including women, joined the armies. The Scythians had a reputation of being invincible, as historical sources often said that the Scythians could not be defeated without outside help. They were known for their horse-riding skills and the use of bows from horseback. The Scythians were an aggressive people, and many became mercenaries. They often used barbed and poisoned arrows in their battles as well.

The Scythian religion was pre-Zoroastrian in nature and was related to the Proto-Indo-Iranian religion. It also may have influenced Slavic, Hungarian, and Turkic mythology. The Scythians worshiped seven gods and goddesses. However, eight of them are mentioned by Herodotus, who claimed these were gods worshiped by the royal family. First amongst them was Tabiti, the queen of gods and protector of homes. Later she was transformed into Atar or Agni, a fire deity of Zoroastrian origin. The Scythians offered animal sacrifices to their gods, with the most prestigious sacrificial animal being the horse. The Scythians also allowed a certain caste of priests, the Enarei, to play a significant role in the political life of the lands. It was believed that these priests received a divine gift directly from the gods and were able to foresee the future. The Enarei used strips made out of linden tree bark to read the future, and they were known to dress in female garments.

Scythian art was known for its small objects, such as jewelry made out of gold. During the early period of Scythian art, they were modeling animal figures, presenting them in combat poses. Art historians suggest that Scythian art was mainly influenced by the Near East during their military expeditions in these regions. It is commonly thought that Scythian art originated from the eastern part of the Eurasian Steppe, which was mainly under Chinese influence. During the sixth century, their artwork started depicting mythological creatures as a result of direct Greek influence. Early Scythian art often presents warriors with almond-shaped eyes using composite bows. Later, under the influence of Greek and Persian art, the warriors in Scythian art started having rounder eyes and longer beards and mustaches. During the Scythian golden age, the Greeks were the ones hired to produce their art. The Greeks crafted objects that represented Scythian legends or were used in religious rituals. By the end of the third century BCE, original Scythian art disappeared under the pressure of Hellenic culture. However, the Scythians continued to produce anthropomorphic gravestones.

Herodotus notes the royal lineage of Scythian King Idanthyrsus, stating that his father was Saulius, his grandfather Gnouros, great-grandfather Lykos, and his great-great-grandfather was Spargapeiths. Herodotus also speaks of Anacharsis, who came from the same royal family and was the brother to Saulius and the son of Gnouros. Anacharsis was a Scythian wiseman who traveled from the northern Black Sea all the way to Athens, where he became a renowned figure of "barbarian wisdom." He became popular in Greek literature, where he is numbered as one of "seven sages." Ephorus, another Greek historian, used the image of Anacharsis to describe his idealized image of the Scythians. There is no historical evidence of any existence of Anacharsis, who was a Hellenized Scythian prince, but the possibility is there. Even Herodotus admits that the Scythians had no knowledge of Anacharsis' existence. Everything we know about this mysterious figure comes from Greek sources and literature, and there is no mention of this persona in Scythian history.

What we do know about Scythian history is that Darius' campaign into the Scythian lands led to a political consolidation amongst the Scythians and their neighbors. Scythian power grew considerably, and in the 490s, they launched an expedition into Thrace, reaching Chersonesos. In Thrace, the Odrysian Kingdom put up a resistance against the Scythian invasion, and new borders between the two dynasties were set. There are records of marriages between the Scythian and Odrysian royal families. For example, the Scythian king Oktamasades was the son of an Odrysian princess.

At that time, the Scythians chose to expand their lands north and northwest, where they destroyed several fortified cities and subjugated the citizens of the Odrysian Kingdom. They also tried for the first time to conquer the Greek colonies in the Pontic regions. Because of their previous friendly relations, the Greek settlements had no fortifications or walls to protect them. This resulted in the abandonment and total destruction of some cities but also in the quick fortification of others. Eventually, the Scythians were successful in having control over various Greek colonies. Herodotus confirms that King Scyles of the Scythians had a residence in Olbia. In Nikonion, for instance, coins that bore the name of Scyles were found.

At this point in history, during the 5th century, a change was happening in the Scythian Empire. With their increasing power, their wealth grew as well. The Greeks mentioned the existence of two Scythian kingdoms, Scythia Minor in today's Romania and Bulgaria, and Greater Scythia, which extended from the Danube to the lower Don Basin. Because of the vast lands that they controlled, the Scythians developed a division of responsibilities inside the empire. They had all the political and military power, but they left the urban citizens to deal with trade themselves, no matter what ethnic group they belonged to. The locals were also responsible for all the manual labor. The Scythians obtained much of their riches through slave trade, over which they had full control.

The Scythians were successful in conquering the Greek colonies to some extent, but the Greeks quickly united against them and formed an alliance under the leadership of the city of Panticapaeum. This alliance of Greek city-states later developed into the Bosporus Kingdom, also known as Cimmerian Bosporus. The Greek colonies that fell under Scythian rule started rebelling and gained their freedom. In the lower Don River territories, a Scythian settlement known as Elizavetovka was established. The Scythians wanted to continue their trade with the Greeks, so they allowed a Greek minority to inhabit this city, but the Scythians took trading, for the most part, of this city into their own hands. Even with a lack of evidence, some archeological sites allow us to assume that the Scythians were suffering some internal struggles. A related Iranian people, known as the Sarmatians, began invading from the east and conquered some Scythian territories. The Sarmatians intermingled with the Scythians, and although it seems they destabilized the political power of Scythia, the situation grew calmer over time.

During the fourth century BCE, Scythian culture blossomed. Most of the known monuments are dated to these times. Of the 2,300 discovered monuments in the steppes the Scythians lived, 2,000 belonged to the fourth century. The burial mounds archeologists found were also the richest during this period. Good relations with the new Bosporan Kingdom influenced the rapid Hellenization of the Scythians, especially the royal family and nobles.

The political life of the Scythians during the fourth century is mostly tied to King Ateas, who ruled sometime between 429 and 339 BCE. He united the Scythian tribes under his rule while invading Thrace at the same time. Ateas allied himself with the Macedonians and successfully conquered Triballoi and Istrianoi. His expansion toward the west caused a conflict with Philip II of Macedon, even though they were often allies. In 339, Philip launched a military campaign against the Scythians, and King Ateas died in battle. With his death, the Scythian Empire disintegrated, even though the Scythian people continued to exist. Alexander the Great continued his father's struggles against them after Philip's death.

A general of Alexander the Great, Zopyrion, led a campaign against the Scythians in 331/30. His army counted 30,000 men when it reached Olba and besieged it. However, they were unable to take the city, and they had to retreat. Zopyrion himself died during this battle.

One more Scythian king is mentioned in history from this period. His name was Agaros, and he was probably meddling in the civil war of the Bosporan Kingdom, where two brothers fought for the throne in 310/9 BCE. He allied himself with Satyros II, who was defeated during this war. Agaros gave refuge to the son of Satyros, Paerisades. Nothing else is known about his rule, but the fact that he intervened in the internal struggles of the Bosporan Kingdom may indicate he ruled over the Crimean steppes, which bordered the Bosporus.

At the beginning of the third century, Scythian culture suddenly disappears from the North Pontic region. The reason is unknown, but there are many speculations, from climate change to economic collapse. The third century was truly a dark age for the Scythians. They were expelled from the Balkans by the Celts, while in the east, the Sarmatians were expanding, slowly overwhelming them. In turn, the Scythians focused on the Greek cities of Crimea. By the middle of the third century, Chersonesos lost all of its settlements in northwestern Crimea.

The Scythians of the second century BCE only inhabited the territories of Crimea, the lower lands of the Dnieper River, and Dobruja. These territories were now known as Scythia Minor. The Scythians returned to their nomadic way of life, but they were also intermingling with the local populations. They established a new kingdom between the Dnieper River and Crimea during this period, and Scythian Neapolis became its capital.

This new Scythian kingdom was Hellenic in nature and even resembled the Greek monarchies instead of the fourth century

Scythian kingdom of nomads. The kingdom had a habit of tying themselves to the Bosporan Kingdom through marriages. The most widely known Scythian king of the late period was Skilurus, and he reigned around 125 BCE. He ruled not only Crimea but also some of the territories of the northwestern Pontic region. He continued to be hostile toward Chersonesos and attacked it, but his army had to retreat when faced by King Mithridates VI of Pontus. A general of Mithridates' army, Diophantus, successfully campaigned against the last Scythian king, Palakos, the son of Skilurus. It took Diophantus three campaigns, which took place between 110 and 107, to completely wipe out the Scythians from their territory, and they even took their capital city. Now, only the Scythians of Dobruja existed, but they were of far less interest to anyone. Eventually, Scythia Minor fell under the rule of Mithridates VI.

The Scythians continued to exist after this, but they renounced their nomadic way of life entirely and began settling themselves. In the first century CE, the Scythians grew in strength enough to attack Chersonesos, which asked Rome for help. Rome easily defeated the Scythians, and they never allowed them to return to this region again. During this period, the Romans mention the Tauro-Scythians, who historians recognize as being a mixed population of the Crimean region. From these times, many Greek and Roman historians use the term Scythian to describe any nomadic people who were of Slavic or Turkish origin.

Chapter 7 – The Persians

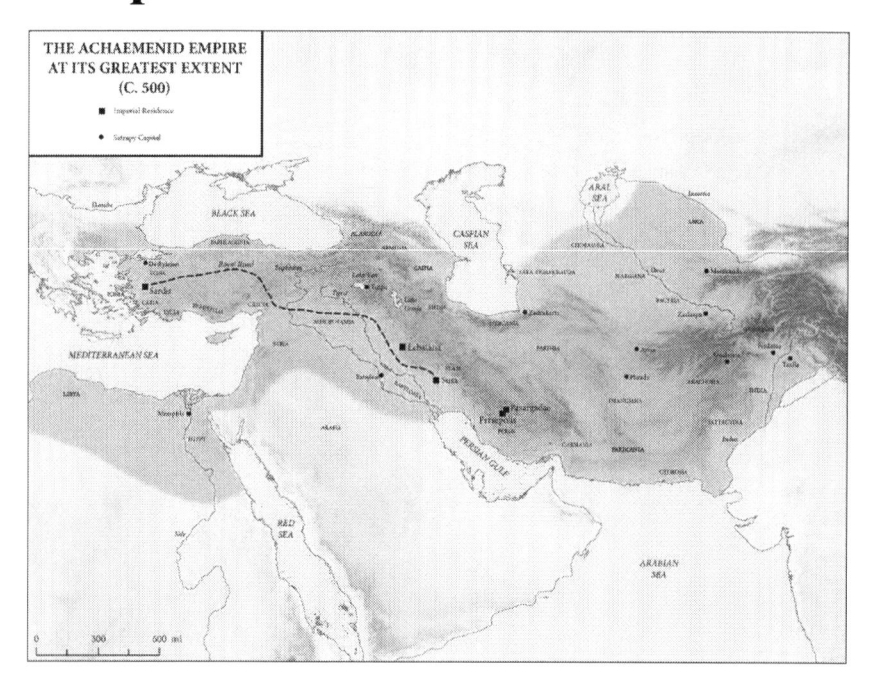

Map of the Achaemenid Empire at its greatest extent

The ancient Persians belonged to the group of Iranian peoples who inhabited the Persis region in southwestern Iran, today known as the Fars Province. There is little information about the first centuries of their history, which was between 1000 and 600 BCE. The first appearance of Persia in old documents is of Assyrian origin from the third millennium BCE. It is written in the old Assyrian form as Parahse, indicating the region that was inhabited by the Sumerians. The Iranian nomadic tribe from this region migrated west of Lake Urmia, taking the name of their homeland with them. Eventually, they were called Persians, and the land they occupied became known as Persis, what historians call Persia proper and the heartland of the later Persian Empire. At first, these nomadic Persians were influenced by the Assyrians, who had ruled them for over three centuries. However, a new power rose in the region.

Medes, another group of Iranian people, organized their own kingdom known as Media, uniting the region against Assyrian rule. Media became a political and cultural power in this region by 612 BCE. In 552, Persis, under the Achaemenid dynasty, was Media's vassal state. Soon after, though, in 550, they rebelled against Media and not only gained their independence but also conquered Media. The first Persian king, who is credited as being the founder of the Persian Empire, was Cyrus the Great, or Cyrus II, who ruled from 600 to 530. The Persian Empire was formed in 550 after the rebellion Cyrus II organized against Media. He had help from various nobles of the Median court and the commander of the Median armies, Harpagus, in overthrowing King Astyages.

Cyrus the Great commanded all of the vassal states that used to bow before Media. His uncle Arsames was the ruler of the city of Parsa, and he willingly gave up his throne to Cyrus. This is how Cyrus managed to unite two kingdoms ruled by the same Achaemenid dynasty. Parsa and Anshan became Persia.

The king of Lydia, Croesus, planned to take advantage of the unrests in the Median kingdom and seize some of its territories for himself, but he had to face a counterattack organized by Cyrus the Great. The exact year of these actions is unknown, but speculations place it in 547 due to information provided by the Nabonidus Chronicle. The Lydians attacked the city of Pteria in Cappadocia, which they besieged and captured. In response, the Persians invited the citizens of Lydia to revolt against Croesus, but they refused. Cyrus decided to lead an army and march against Lydians. His army gained numbers as he recruited more men from the nations he passed through on his way to Pteria. Neither side won in the battle, and both the Persians and the Lydians suffered great losses. King Croesus was forced to retreat back to his capital in Sardis.

Croesus called for his allies to help him, but Cyrus attacked again by the end of winter, so Croesus' allies had no time to send aid. The Persians besieged Sardis for fourteen days when Croesus finally decided to meet Cyrus in open battle, known as the Battle of Thymbra. The battle took place on the northern plains of Sardis, and the Lydian army outnumbered the Persians two to one. However, Harpagus, the renegade Median commander who still advised Cyrus, pushed to put camels in the front row in order to confuse the Lydian cavalry, whose horses were not used to the smell. This proved to be a tactic that decided the fate of the battle. The Persians won, and Sardis fell. Herodotus writes that Cyrus spared Croesus and made him his own advisor, but this information contradicts the Nabonidus Chronicle, which states that the Lydian king was killed. Nabonidus, who the chronicle was named after, was a Babylonian king who also suffered from a Persian invasion led by Cyrus. As it is from the same period, historians are inclined to trust his chronicle more than Herodotus' version of history.

The Persian commander Mazares, a former Median general, was entrusted with dealing with small uprisings in Lydia. After Lydia was subdued, Mazares continued into the Greek territories, where he took the cities of Magnesia and Priene. He continued his conquest in Ionia but soon after died of unknown causes. Harpagus was sent to finish the conquest of Asia Minor, and he captured Lycia, Cilicia, and Phoenicia. After ending his campaigns, he returned to Persia in 542.

In the winter of 540, Cyrus conquered Elam and took its capital, Susa. He continued to the city of Opis on the Tigris River, situated just north of Babylon, where he forced the Babylonian army to retreat. On October 10th, 539, he conquered the city of Sippar, where the Babylonian king Nabonidus resided. However, the king fled to the capital city, Babylon. Only two days later, the Persians entered Babylon; its citizens showed no resistance, and the Persians captured King Nabonidus. When Cyrus entered Babylon on October 29th, it proclaimed the end of the Neo-Babylonian Empire. With the fall of Babylonia, the Persians gained all of the territories this empire possessed, including Syria and Judah.

With the fall of Babylonia, Cyrus became the king of the largest empire the world had ever seen at the time. His empire occupied territories from Asia Minor in the west to the Indus River in the east. In the Cyrus Cylinder, a declaration made on a clay cylinder after the fall of Babylonia, Cyrus claims he improved the lives of his citizens. He repatriated the displaced peoples and worked on restoring the temples and sanctuaries. Some historians regard this cylinder as the first document describing human rights, but the majority sees it in the context of new policies of Mesopotamian kings who began their reign with announcing reforms to the kingdom.

There are many sources that describe the death of Cyrus the Great, but they all differ from each other. Some say he died during the invasion of Massagetae, a tribe that lived in the southern parts of modern Kazakhstan, and others say he died peacefully in his capital city. Furthermore, there are records of Cyrus being killed by his wife Tomyris, who was also the queen of Massagetae. And finally, the Greek historian Ctesias claims Cyrus died while quelling a rebellion that happened in the northeastern regions of the River Syr. The common belief is that the remains of Cyrus the Great were buried in the capital city of Pasargadae.

The second king of the Achaemenid Empire was Cyrus' son, Cambyses II, who ruled from 530 to 522. Even though his reign was brief, he is known for conquering territories in Africa, particularly Egypt. But before he became king of the vast Persian Empire, he was appointed as the governor of Babylonia. When his father, Cyrus the Great, decided to march against Massagetae, he became co-ruler and eventually the sole ruler after his father's death.

Cambyses didn't have trouble ascending to the throne, as the empire was stable, so all he had to do was preserve his authority over Persia's vast territories. The last prominent power in the Near East at the time was Egypt, and Cambyses took it upon himself to conquer it. Hearing of Persia's aspiration to take Egypt, some of the allies of Pharaoh Ahmose II (Amasis II) decided to abandon him and join forces with Cambyses. Egypt's former ally, Polycrates, the Greek king of Samos (better known as the tyrant of Samos), helped the Persians capture Cyprus, which was under Egyptian rule. This turned out to be a heavy blow to Ahmose II. Soon after, the pharaoh died and was succeeded by his son, Psamtik III, who only ruled for six months before facing the Persians and losing the Battle of Pelusium in 525. This battle took place at the eastern edge of the Nile Delta, and records say that the Egyptians had a strong defense, but the Persians were, nonetheless, victorious. Psamtik ran to Memphis, where he tried to resist the siege, but soon after, he was captured and carried in chains to Susa, where he committed suicide.

After the fall of Egypt, the Lydians and Greeks of Cyrene and Barca acknowledged Persian rule without resistance. Showing generosity, Cyrene allowed the widow of Pharaoh Ahmose II, who was Greek, to return to her home in Cyrene. To present his conquest of Egypt as legitimate, Cambyses used propaganda to claim he was of Egyptian origin, that he was the son of Princess Nitetis, daughter of Pharaoh Apries. Furthermore, he took titles belonging to the previous Egyptian pharaoh, naming himself the "King of Upper and Lower Egypt."

Cambyses had to leave Egypt in the spring of 522 to deal with a rebellion in Persia. While traversing Syria, he was wounded, and the wound turned gangrenous. Cambyses died three weeks later, and he left his empire without a direct successor. So, the throne was taken by his younger brother, Bardiya.

Bardiya was known to the Greeks as Smerdis, and allegedly, he ruled for only a few months. The story of Bardiya's rule has many variations according to different sources. Darius the Great claims that Bardiya was killed by his brother, King Cambyses II, who did it to ensure his position on the throne. Herodotus claims Bardiya was assassinated later during the invasion of Egypt and that an impostor took his place in court. They both agree that a certain mage-priest from Media impersonated Bardiya and took the throne. It seems that sources do not agree on the name of this mage as Darius calls him Gaumata, Herodotus Oropastes, and according to Ctesias, his name was Sphendadates. A group of seven Persian nobles discovered that the new king was an impostor and plotted to kill him. He was stabbed to death in September of 522. Not much is known about the rule of the imposter Bardiya, but some records mention his exemption of taxes for three years, which was probably why nobody rebelled against him.

Today, historians are inclined to believe that the usurper Gaumata, was actually the real throne successor, known to history as King Bardiya. Darius himself came up with the story of the mage who came from Media and became the pretend ruler to justify the assassination of the original king and make his coup legitimate. Several days after Gaumata was killed, Darius was crowned in Pasargadae.

Darius I, also known as Darius the Great, ruled as the fourth king of the Achaemenid Empire from 550 until 486 BCE. During his rule, the empire was at its peak. It included the territories of West and Central Asia, the Caucasus, the Balkans, the coast of the Black Sea, the Indus Valley, Egypt, and the northern parts of Africa, eastern Libya, and Sudan's coast.

Darius was a son of a noble who served in the Persian court. Herodotus mentions he was a *doryphoros*, a spearman of Cambyses II. Many historians interpret this as being the king's personal spear-carrier.

Herodotus provides an improbable story of Darius' ascension. To decide who would take the crown after the assassination of Gaumata, Darius and six other nobles agreed on taking a test. Each one of them would ride on his horse outside of the palace walls at sunrise. The noble whose horse would be the first to neigh, greeting the sunrise, would become the new monarch. The story goes that a slave called Oebares rubbed his hand over the genitals of a mare and approached Darius' horse, which became excited by the smell and neighed first. The clouds thundered at the same time, and the other six nobles dismounted, kneeling in front of their new king. Herodotus continues the story with Darius erecting a statue of himself, which presents Darius on a neighing horse with the inscription "Darius, son of Hystaspes, obtained the sovereignty of Persia by the sagacity of his horse and the ingenious contrivance of Oebares, his groom." Herodotus is known for often mixing folklore with history; therefore, this story is considered an unlikely one, albeit an interesting one.

After the coronation, Darius had to face a number of revolts across the country, as Bardiya had many supporters. Elam and Babylonia were the first to rebel, but Darius had no problem ending these revolts, as it took him only three months to end the Babylonian resistance. Soon after, there was a revolution in Bactria, Persis, Media, Parthia, Assyria, and Egypt. By 522, almost the whole empire was in revolt against Darius. However, with his loyal army, Darius had no problem suppressing the revolts and rebellions in just one year.

In 515, Darius launched a campaign to conquer the Indus Valley, continuing where his predecessor Cyrus had stopped in 535 BCE. The exact areas he conquered during this expedition are not known, as Darius himself writes it as the lands of Hindush. Modern scholars propose this area to be in the middle and lower Indus Valley, but there is no archeological evidence of Persians being there.

In 513, Darius had to turn his attention toward the Scythians, who threatened to close the trade routes between Central Asia and the shores of the Black Sea. Darius crossed the Black Sea with his army, using bridges made out of boats. But before entering Scythia, he conquered most of Eastern Europe. The Scythians undertook scorched-earth tactics as they retreated, but the Persian army followed the Scythians in their retreat, hoping to engage in open battle.

Toward the end of his campaign in the Scythian lands, Darius ordered eight forts to be built, with a distance from each other of eight miles. These forts were the frontier defense, marking the end of his progression in Scythia. However, he abandoned this project due to the winter that was coming. In order not to lose any more troops, Darius turned his army toward Thrace. He had failed to bring the Scythians into open combat, but the Scythians failed as well by losing a great deal of land to the Persians. Darius couldn't secure the territories he conquered in Scythia, and he never returned to them. This campaign turned out to be a very expensive stalemate.

The Greeks living in Asia Minor submitted to the Persians by 510, but there were also pro-Persian Greeks in Athens. In order to attract Greek traders, Darius opened his court to all those who wanted to come and serve Persia. The Greeks came and served as soldiers, statesmen, and artisans, but back home, the remaining Greek power was concerned about the strength of Darius' empire. This concern would culminate into a conflict between some Greek cities and the Achaemenid Empire.

The first to revolt was Miletus, under the leadership of its ruler Aristagoras. Soon after, Eretria and Athens joined and sent their troops and ships to help Miletus. They burned the city of Sardis, but the Persians responded fast and were able to reoccupy the Ionian and Greek islands. Thrace and Macedon declared independence, but that didn't last long. In 492, the Persians managed to quickly take control of them. Until then, Macedon was a Persian vassal state that had always kept its autonomy. It was only after the last conquest that it was brought entirely under the Achaemenid Empire. As a result of the Ionian revolts, anti-Persian parties gained popularity in Athens and Sparta, and they expelled their political opponents who were pro-Persian. Darius responded to this by sending an army across the Dardanelles. However, the Thracians blocked their way by harassing them until they chose to return to Persia. Darius, in his anger, gathered a larger army of 20,000 men under the joint command of Median admiral Datis and Persian general Artaphernes, who were successful and captured Eretria. In 490, the Persians met the Athenian army at the Battle of Marathon. The Persians were defeated, and this event marked the end of the first invasion of the Achaemenid Empire into Greece.

Darius had spent three years preparing a second invasion into the Greek territory; he even planned to lead the expedition himself instead of giving the command to others. But Egypt revolted, which affected Darius' health considerably. In October of 486, Darius the Great died. He was embalmed and buried at Naqsh-e Rostam, a necropolis he built about twelve kilometers (about a little over a mile) from his royal capital of Persepolis.

Darius I was succeeded by his son, Xerxes I, or Xerxes the Great. His name translates to "He who rules over heroes," and like his father, he ruled the Achaemenid Empire when it was at its peak, ruling from 486 to 465. In the Bible, he is mentioned under the name of Ahasuerus.

Xerxes was the child of Darius and Atossa, who was the daughter of the first king, Cyrus the Great. This fact helped Xerxes gain the throne as he was not the oldest child. His half-brother Artobazan wanted the crown for himself as he was the oldest of all the siblings. However, he came from a marriage Darius had with the daughter of his spear-carrier before he ascended to the throne. Xerxes received help from the Spartan king who was in exile in Persia, Demaratus, who argued that it is the first son born in a royal marriage that had the claim to the throne, which meant that it didn't necessarily mean the oldest son. Xerxes was crowned in October 486, and he was around 36 years old at the time. His ascension to the throne was smooth due to his mother's power, which not even Artobazan dared to challenge.

Soon after the crowning ceremony, Xerxes crushed a rebellion in Egypt by stationing his brother Achaemenes as the governor there.

In 484, Xerxes confiscated a golden statue of Bel (Marduk) from Babylonia and melted it. This action outraged the Babylonians, who rebelled for the next two years.

During the rule of Darius I, the Athenians, Naxians, and Eretrians interfered in the Ionian Revolt, but due to his father's death, it was up to Xerxes to punish them. Xerxes started the preparation for the second invasion of Greece in 483 and ordered the digging of a canal through the isthmus of Mount Athos. At first, some Greek cities willingly joined Xerxes, such as Thessaly, Thebes, and Argos. Xerxes initiated the attacks on the Greek territories in 480, and the Persians were victorious in these battles, partly because Xerxes led the Persian army himself.

Herodotus exaggerates the numbers of his army to be over a million men, but modern scholars estimate it at being roughly 60,000. Herodotus also names the Persian elite infantry as the Immortals and claims Xerxes had 10,000 of them. The Immortals served as an elite imperial guard but also as a standing army, waiting to be called to battle if needed. They played an important role in the upcoming battle against the Greeks.

Xerxes is probably known the most for his role in the Battle of Thermopylae, which took place over the course of three days in August or September of 480 BCE. The allied forces of the Greek cities, under the leadership of the Spartan king Leonidas, clashed with the Persian armies of Xerxes I at the pass of Thermopylae. The initial idea of the Greek general Themistocles was to block the Persian advantage at the pass of Thermopylae and to simultaneously fight the Persian navy in the shallow waters of Artemisium, a cape in northern Euboea, Greece.

The Persian army marched toward Greece and was met by 7,000 Greek men who were blocking the pass. The Greek army was vastly outnumbered, as the Persian force numbered anywhere between 60,000 and 150,000, but they endured for seven days (only three days had actual fighting). After the second day of battle, a Greek soldier named Ephialtes betrayed his countrymen and revealed to the Persians a small path that would lead them right behind the Greek forces. Realizing his armies were outflanked, Leonidas chose to stand his position and fight to the death together with 300 Spartans and 700 Thespians, who guarded the retreat of the rest of Greece's army. There were reports of other members of the Greek allied forces standing their ground with the Spartans and Thespians, like the helots and Thebans, but they surrendered almost immediately.

At the same time, a naval battle took place at Artemisium, where the Greek army under Themistocles blocked the passage of the Persian armada. Upon hearing that the pass of Thermopylae was lost, Themistocles chose to retreat; in order for Greece's tactics to work, they would need both passes to be held. The Greek ships withdraw to the island of Salamis, and the Persians then overran the region of Boeotia and also captured Phocis, Attica, and Euboea. However, the Greek fleet attacked the Persians at the Battle of Salamis and won.

In order to avoid being trapped in Europe where he had no footholds, Xerxes had to return his forces to Asia. He lost most of his army due to starvation and disease. He left Mardonius, a military commander, with part of the Persian army to complete the invasion of Greece, but the very next year, the Greek army completely wiped out the Persians at the Battle of Plataea. This battle ended the Persian invasion.

The Battle of Thermopylae was an example of patriotism in modern and ancient literature. Even though greatly romanticized, this battle was a symbol of love for one's country and one's will to defend it. This battle is by far one of the most famous military clashes in ancient European history, as it is referenced in all spheres of culture, whether ancient or recent.

Xerxes was known for his rage, and upon retrieving the body of the Spartan king Leonidas, he ordered it to be decapitated and crucified. This was unusual for the Persians since usually they treated their brave and valiant enemies with respect. After the Persians abandoned the pass of Thermopylae, the Greeks returned to bury their fallen soldiers and to erect a statue of a lion dedicated to Leonidas. It took forty years for the Spartans to retrieve the bones of their king and give him a proper burial with full honors. In his memory, they started a tradition of funeral games being held each year.

On top of the burial mound of the Spartans at the site of the battle, a stone with an epitaph was raised to commemorate the event. It is written by Simonides, a Greek poet, and it reads, "Oh stranger, tell the Lacedaemonians that we lie here, obedient to their words." The Greeks often referred to the Spartans as Lacedaemonians because of the name of the region where Sparta was located, and by "obedient to their words," it means that they fought to their death, as they were ordered to by King Leonidas.

Xerxes was assassinated in August 465 by the commander of his royal bodyguards, Artabanus, who had the help of a eunuch serving in the harem. Artabanus planned to overthrow the Achaemenid dynasty, and after the assassination, he placed his own seven sons in key positions at court. Artabanus became the regent of Persia during 465 and 464. It is uncertain whether Artabanus also killed crown prince Darius, the son of Xerxes, or if he accused him of patricide while leaving his execution to the people. However, it is certain that both Xerxes and Darius lost their lives around the same time. The dynasty of Artabanus is uncertain, as some reports claim he named Artaxerxes I as king but acted as the reagent of the empire, while other sources say he claimed the throne for himself, wishing to end the royal dynasty, but due to the betrayal of general Megabyzus, he met his end by the sword of Artaxerxes.

Xerxes I was succeeded by his third son, Artaxerxes I, who ruled from 465 until 424. During his reign, Elamite stopped being the language of the government; instead, the Aramaic language was popularized. In addition, the solar calendar replaced the old national calendar while he was the king. The main religion of the state under Artaxerxes was Zoroastrianism.

Early during his rule, Artaxerxes had to deal with uprisings in Egypt, which lasted for six years (460 to 454 BCE). The revolt was led by Inaros II, the son of a Libyan prince. With allies from Athens, Inaros II defeated the Persian army and besieged Memphis. The Persian army under Megabyzus ended the siege of the city, defeating Inaros in 454, who was captured and delivered to Susa, where he was executed.

Artaxerxes continued his father's ambition to conquer the whole of Greece, and he employed new tactics against Athens. He funded Athens' enemies in hopes of weakening it enough that it would surrender. However, this strategy sparked a series of conflicts. The Greeks formed the Delian League in 478 during the second Persian invasion, which was an alliance of 150 to 300 Greek cities under the leadership of Athens. Wars fought between the League and the Achaemenid Empire were just a continuation of the Greco-Persian Wars started by Darius I. In 451, the Delian League attacked Cyprus under the command of Cimon, an Athenian general. Their fleet numbered 200 ships of Athenians and their allies. They besieged the city-state of Kition in Cyprus, where Cimon died. Because of a lack of provisions, the League had to retreat toward Salamis. The Persians attacked the League's forces that were leaving Cimon by sea as well as by land. The League was ultimately victorious, and with the defeat of Artaxerxes' armies, the end of the Greco-Persian Wars was finally achieved in 449. A peace treaty was signed by both parties, and it included the autonomy of all Greek cities, as well as forbidding Persian armies from entering Greek lands or maritime territories. Furthermore, the Athenians were not to send troops into Persian territories.

Artaxerxes I died in 424 and was immediately succeeded by his only legitimate son, Xerxes II, who was assassinated after 45 days by his half-brother, Sogdianus, who ruled for a little over six months. Sogdianus met his end by the hand of his half-brother Ochus, who took the name Darius II upon his crowning.

Darius II ruled the Achaemenid Empire from 423 to 404. There are not many resources that describe the reign of Darius II. It is known there was a rebellion led by the people of Medes in 409, and a mention of Darius' name in harem intrigues. Some sources depict him as being dependent on his wife Parysatis, an illegitimate daughter of Artaxerxes I, with whom Darius had four sons. Her favorite son of all four was Cyrus, and she used her influence to give him command over western Anatolia while he was in his early teenage years.

Darius II commanded his satraps in Asia Minor, Tissaphernes and Pharnabazus, to attack Athens. The Persian satraps allied themselves with Sparta and started a war, which ended in Athens' defeat in 404. Under Darius, Persia managed to conquer a large part of Ionia. However, soon after, Darius II died in Babylon of illness. While he was on his deathbed, his wife Parysatis begged him to crown his second eldest son, her favorite Cyrus, but he refused.

Artaxerxes II instead inherited the throne, and he arrested his younger brother Cyrus, who was plotting to assassinate him. He was preparing to execute Cyrus when their mother intervened and begged for Artaxerxes to spare his brother's life. Cyrus was spared and given control over Lydia, where he prepared a rebellion. He employed Greek mercenaries known as the "Ten Thousand" to take his brother's throne for him.

The Ten Thousand fought at the Battle of Cunaxa against the Persians in 401. Xenophon, a Greek historian, reports that the Persians were scared of the mercenaries and that by the end of the battle, the Ten Thousand had only one wounded man. However, Cyrus died in that battle, and having no employer, the mercenaries decided to end the campaign and turn back to Greece. At first, they tried to find a new employer who would hire them to finish the job Cyrus started. They offered their services to Ariaeus, a general that was allied with them, but he refused, stating that he could not be the Persian king as he was not of royal blood. The Ten Thousand then approached Tissaphernes, the satrap of Lydia, but he refused them, too. In order to avoid conflict with the mercenaries, Tissaphernes funded their way home.

Artaxerxes involved himself in a new war against the Spartans, the Corinthian War, which lasted from 395 to 387. Agesilaus II, the Spartan king, began invading Asia Minor in 396. Artaxerxes then bribed the Greek states, particularly Athens, Thebes, and Corinth, in order to start a war with Sparta. These bribes were paid in darics, the main currency of the Achaemenid Empire, and they were the means of starting the Corinthian War. At the Battle of Cnidus in 394, the Persians, with the help of allied Athens, managed to defeat the Spartan fleet. The Persians increased pressure on Sparta by raiding the Peloponnesian coast. Athens felt strong enough to return some of the Greek cities of Asia Minor back under their fold. However, this worried Artaxerxes, as Athens' power suddenly grew.

In 386, Artaxerxes made a deal with Sparta and betrayed his allies. In the Treaty of Antalcidas, which ended the Corinthian War in 387, he forced his former allies to return the former Greek city-states of Ionia and Aeolis in Anatolia to the Achaemenid Empire. He also gave Sparta the power over the Greek mainland territories.

In 385, Artaxerxes undertook a campaign against the Cadusii, an ancient Iranian tribe. The sources do not offer reasons for this campaign, but it is believed it was to stop a revolt and make them pay tribute to Persia. Plutarch, a Greek biographer, describes this campaign, saying that the Persian army, numbering around 300,000 infantry and 10,000 cavalries, went deep into Cadusii land, but the mountainous region of these lands had no food to sustain such an army. Soon, they began to starve. At first, they ate their supplies, but later, they had to eat their own mounts. Tiribazus, a Persian general, came up with the idea to divide the Cadusii tribes, convincing their leaders that their opponents sent envoys to join the Persian army. They all submitted to Artaxerxes, which ended the Cadusian campaign.

During the reign of Artaxerxes II, Egypt managed to regain its independence. It all began with a revolt that was organized during the first years of his reign. In 373, Artaxerxes sent an expedition to regain Egypt, led by Pharnabazus, a satrap of Phrygia, and Iphicrates, an Athenian general who commanded a group of mercenaries. Due to the distrust between the two generals and the annual flooding of the Nile, the Persians lost what was supposed to be an easy victory. This event was the end of Pharnabazus' career. The second expedition to Egypt was led by Datames, a satrap of Cappadocia, but he, too, failed.

This defeat in Egypt was the spark that ignited unrest among the Achaemenid nobility. In 372, this unrest culminated with the Great Satraps' Revolt against Artaxerxes. Datames, the satrap who was sent for the second attempt to regain Egypt, suddenly felt exposed to too much risk at the royal court because of his opponent's machinations. He abandoned his loyalty to the Persian king and started a revolt by returning to Cappadocia with his troops. He managed to persuade the satraps from within Persia to revolt as well. Egypt was openly financing this rebellion against Artaxerxes, but the Persian king was successful in ending it by 362. Not long after these events, legend has it that Artaxerxes II died of a broken heart caused by the behavior of his sons.

When Artaxerxes II died in 358, he was succeeded by his son Artaxerxes III, who ruled until 338 BCE. He came to power after his older brother was executed and the other one had committed suicide. To secure his crown, Artaxerxes III murdered over eighty members of his family.

Upon taking the throne, Artaxerxes III had to deal with the rebellion of Artabazus II, the satrap of Phrygia, who gathered allies and fought for independence. Among the allies of Artabazus were Athens, Thebe, and Mysia, and with such a force, Artabazus managed to defeat the royal Persian army in 354. But the very next year, Artaxerxes' army came back and defeated Artabazus, who sought refuge with Philip II of Macedon.

In 351, Artaxerxes launched a new campaign to recover Egypt. After a year of fighting the Egyptian pharaoh, Nectanebo II, the Persians suffered defeat and were forced to retreat. At the same time, an uprising in Asia Minor broke out, and Artaxerxes had to abandon his plans of retaking Egypt, at least for the time being.

The rebellions in Cyprus and Sidon had a goal of making their states independent. They had some success in the early stages of their uprising when they defeated the Persian army led by Idieus, the satrap of Caria. But after this defeat, Artaxerxes gathered a large army of over 300,000 men, including a number of mercenaries he hired and the Greek armies who came to help. The Persian king was successful this time, and he managed to completely crush the rebellion. Sidon was burned to the ground, but the sources are not clear whether the Persian army burned the city or harmed its citizens. The estimations are that there were at least 40,000 civilian deaths, though. After the fall of Sidon, Artaxerxes sold its ruins to speculators who hoped to dig out various treasures from the ashes.

After ending the rebellion, Artaxerxes returned to his plans to retake Egypt. In 343, he gathered an army of 330,000 Persians, 14,000 Greeks, 4,000 mercenaries, 3,000 men sent by Argos, and 1,000 from Thebes. Pharaoh Nectanebo II managed to resist this army for some time with his 100,000 men. His tactical position gave him a good fighting chance, but the pharaoh did not have generals capable of leading his army, so he was defeated. Nectanebo fled to Memphis and then continued to Ethiopia. After conquering Egypt, Artaxerxes started looting its temples and terrorizing its citizens. He raised taxes on Egypt and persecuted its native religion in hopes of weakening it so they would never again revolt against the Achaemenid Empire. Egypt stayed under Persian control for the next ten years until Alexander the Great finally conquered it.

Artaxerxes spent the last years of his reign in peace, as there were no rebellions in his empire. However, the power Philip II of Macedon managed to gather called for a Persian response. Artaxerxes tried influencing the neighbors of Macedon in an effort to constrain

Philip's power, but Philip had already started planning the invasion of Persia. He was just waiting for the Greeks to join him as allies.

Artaxerxes III died of natural causes in 338, although a Greek source by Diodorus of Sicily claims it was from poisoning by a eunuch named Bagoas and his own physician.

The next king of the Achaemenid Empire was Artaxerxes IV, also known as Arses (ruled 338 to 336). He was the youngest son of Artaxerxes III, but since all of his older brothers had died before he became king, Arses became the new king. It is believed that the eunuch Bagoas wanted to become a kingmaker, so he placed young Arses on the throne, believing he could control the inexperienced king. Being unsuccessful in controlling him, Bagoas decided to poison Arses as well and placed Darius III on the throne, Arses' cousin. During this time, Philip II of Macedon gained the alliance he sought from the Greeks in his plans to invade Persia.

Darius III ruled from 380 until July 330 BCE. Greek historians say he poisoned Bagoas and watched him die once he learned of his predecessor's fate. During Darius' rule, the empire was affected by constant rebellions, as the satraps were jealous of each other's power and indulged in scheming and plotting.

In 336, the Hellenic League, also known as the League of Corinth (a confederation of Hellenic states established by Philip II), authorized Philip II of Macedon to launch a military campaign against the Achaemenid Empire for destroying and burning the temples of Athens during the Persian wars that happened over a century before. But Philip's campaign was quickly suspended due to his death. He did manage, however, to recover some Greek cities in Asia Minor that were under Persian rule, but soon after that, he was assassinated.

Philip was succeeded by his son, Alexander the Great, who invaded Asia Minor in 334. He was victorious against the Persians in his very first battles. The Battle of Granicus in 334 BCE was fought near the site of Troy, and it marked the fall of Asia Minor under the rule of Alexander the Great. This was one of the three major battles that led to the fall of the Achaemenid Empire. Darius III did not participate in these first battles, leaving them in the hands of the Persian satraps in Asia Minor. A year later, in 333, Darius appeared at the Battle of Issus, where his forces finally met the Macedonian army of Alexander. Even though the Persians outnumbered their opponents two to one, they were outflanked and forced to retreat. However, the beginning of the battle didn't go so well for Alexander's army. Historians report that the Macedonians lost 128 officers in the first military confrontation. Alexander took control of the battle by mounting his horse and charging directly at Darius and his bodyguards, who were forced to flee. Seeing the Persian king leave, the Greek mercenaries were the first to abandon the battle, followed by the rest of the Persian army. Alexander's cavalry continued to pursue the Persians as long as the day lasted.

Darius' wife, Stateira I, was captured after the battle, as well as her daughters and Darius' mother, who had followed him as he battled throughout the lands. It is said that Alexander treated the captured women with great respect; he even married Darius' daughter, Stateira II. Darius wrote letters to Alexander asking for his family back, but he refused to liberate them for as long as Darius denied acknowledging him as the new king of Persia.

The third and final battle that marked the end of the Persian Empire was fought in 331, and it took place near the city of Gaugamela. Darius' army was greatly outnumbered by the Macedonians, and the initial clashes were in his favor. He was already on the battlefield with his forces, waiting for the arrival of Alexander the Great. Again, Alexander himself led the final charge in the center of the Persian army, and he destroyed Darius' royal guard and forced Darius to run with whatever troops he could gather around him. When he was on the run, Darius gave a speech to encourage his fighters, promising another battle where they would have the opportunity to avenge their loss. He planned to raise another army to help him fight Alexander at Babylon, but his satraps refused to send him any help.

Darius was murdered during the retreat by one of his satraps, Bessus, later known as Artaxerxes V. Upon finding Darius' body, Alexander was disturbed to see his respected enemy killed in such a fashion, and he gave the Persian king a proper burial at Persepolis. The following year Alexander captured and killed Bessus, and the rest of the Persian satraps eventually pledged their loyalty to Alexander. Even though Bessus was a member of the royal family and proclaimed himself the king of kings, Darius is considered to be the last king of the Achaemenid Empire.

Chapter 8 – The Seleucid Empire and Romans in Anatolia

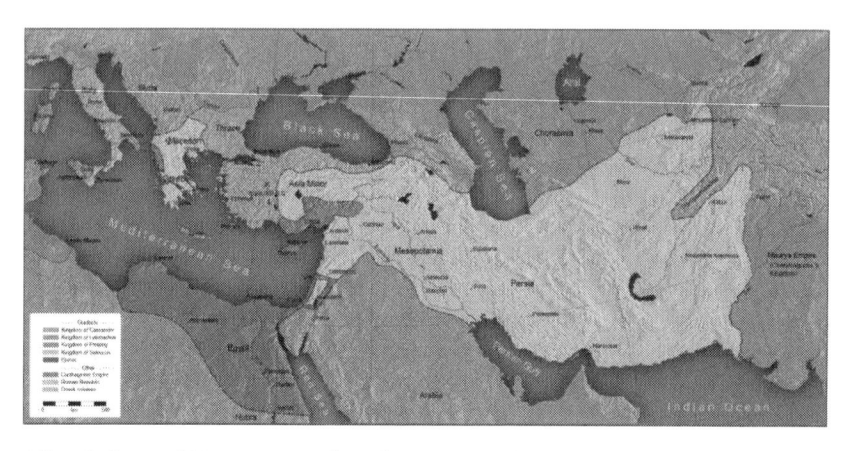

The Seleucid Empire under the reign of Seleucus I Nicator

Alexander the Great died in 323 BCE in the palace of Nebuchadnezzar II, the king of Babylonia. The circumstances of his death are unknown, but he left no successor, although his wife was pregnant at the moment of his death. Alexander's brother was alive at the time, but he wasn't capable of ruling due to his mental health issues. So, forty years of infighting in Macedon followed, as various "successors" fought against each other. The unity of Macedon seized to exist, and the kingdom was finally divided into four smaller ones: Ptolemaic Egypt, Seleucid Mesopotamia and Central Asia, Attalid Anatolia, and Antigonid Macedon.

The Seleucid Empire was founded in 312 by Seleucus I Nicator, whose dynasty ruled the lands until 63 BCE. The Seleucids took control of Babylonia after the division of Macedon, but they expanded into an empire. At its highest, the Seleucid Empire included central Anatolia, Persia, Levant, Mesopotamia, and parts of today's Kuwait, Afghanistan, Pakistan, and Turkmenistan.

In 301, Seleucus I expanded his territories to eastern Anatolia as well as northern Syria. He allied himself with three famous generals who served under Alexander the Great: Lysimachus, Ptolemy, and Cassander, and they went against Antigonus, another general. The wars between them are known as the Wars of the Diadochi, which would determine the boundaries of the new Hellenistic kingdoms. Later, in 281, Seleucus planned to take the territories of his former ally Lysimachus, expanding his kingdom to western Anatolia, but he was assassinated by Ptolemy Keraunos, the second king of Ptolemaic Egypt who also crowned himself king of Macedon.

Previously, Seleucus defeated Lysimachus in the Battle of Corupedium in 281 BCE. Lysimachus' kingdom fell apart, and the capital city of Pergamon was taken by Philetaerus, a nobleman and officer in the Macedonian army. He founded the Attalid dynasty of Pergamon in Anatolia. Even though Pergamon was officially under Seleucid rule, it continued enjoying autonomy under the rule of Philetaerus, as he was the one holding Lysimachus' treasury. He used all the wealth he acquired by taking the city to gain influence and extend his power beyond the city. He defended the city from the Gauls and built fortifications and temples, thus gaining prestige and trust amongst his subjects.

His successor Eumenes I was the one who gained complete independence from the Seleucid Empire in 263 through a series of organized rebellions. He extended the kingdom's borders south of the Caiscus River, all the way to the Gulf of Cyme. During the existence of the Pergamon Kingdom, there were constant wars over territories against the Seleucid Empire, and the kingdom's borders often changed. During the reign of Attalus I, who ruled from 241 to 197, the kingdom lost all of its territories and was reduced to the city of Pergamon. During the First Macedonian War in 214, the Kingdom of Pergamon allied itself with the Romans and supported Rome in all future wars. The last king of the Attalid dynasty, Attalus III, died in 133, leaving his kingdom to the people of the Roman Republic.

Antiochus I Soter, son of Seleucus I, inherited the throne, but he was unable to fulfill his father's plans of expansion. During the reign of Antiochus I Soter and his son Antiochus II Theos, Asia Minor was under constant war. The struggle for territory wasn't just with Ptolemy II of Egypt, as the Celtic invasions started increasing as well. Various provinces managed to gain independence during these times, including Cappadocia, Bactria, and Parthia. Hellenistic culture was blooming in the newly-freed regions, and Bactria even allied itself with the Greeks and formed the Greco-Bactrian Kingdom.

Seleucus II Callinicus, the next successor to the throne, lost even more of the Seleucid territory. Torn between the war against Ptolemy III and a civil war against his own brother, Seleucus II was unable to remain in control in Pergamum. The Attalid dynasty instead ruled in Pergamum once again during the 230s. Even more territories of Asia Minor were lost, and the Gauls settled in Galatia in the highlands of central Anatolia.

However, the son of Seleucus II, Antiochus III the Great, pushed to regain the former territories of the Seleucid Empire. He took the throne in 222, after his brother Seleucus III, and almost immediately began a new war, which he lost. Even though he was defeated on one front, he spent the next ten years being victorious and successful in returning old territories to his kingdom, such as Bactria and Parthia. After subduing these territories, he allied himself with Philip V of Macedon in order to conquer and divide the territories of

Ptolemaic Egypt. During yet another war, which lasted from 202 to 195, Antiochus III defeated Ptolemy V and gained control over Coele-Syria.

This situation did not last for long. Antiochus' ally Philip V was defeated by the Romans in 197, who attacked Macedon, arguing that they were freeing the Greek city-states. Seeing the opportunity to take over some Macedonian territories, Antiochus sent a military force, but Rome created new innovative war tactics that the Seleucid army couldn't match. Antiochus was defeated in two major battles, Thermopylae in 191 and Magnesia in 190. He was forced to sign the Treaty of Apamea in 188 BC and made peace with Rome. The major clause of this treaty was for the Seleucids to completely retreat from Anatolia and never to enter the territories west of the Taurus Mountains again. The former lands of the Seleucid Empire in Anatolia were given to Rome's allies, mainly Rhodes and Pergamum.

This might look like Rome was generous by not taking the Anatolian territories for itself, but by dividing the lands between its allies, Rome made sure none of them would become powerful enough to pose a threat. This way, Rome also ensured it stayed involved in all Anatolian affairs.

The next few decades were quite peaceful in Anatolia, and Rome did not meddle in its affairs to much extent, but it was still a force that protected the freedom of its allies and the new kingdoms that came to be after the Seleucids abandoned these territories. The Galatians were the only remaining problem in Anatolia, as they often organized raids, until the war against Bithynia. At the time, the ruler of Bithynia was Prusias I, who, during the Roman war against Antiochus III, did not want to choose a side, and he actually managed to stay neutral. It is not known what started the war, but it was concluded by 183.

Rome had full control over the rulers in Anatolia, and even though they had no lands of their own, they enacted their influence on the events concerning Anatolia. The first province Rome officially adopted was in 133 when King Attalus III bequeathed Pergamon to the citizens of Rome.

In the year 91 BCE, Rome had to focus its attention on their homeland due to the Social War breaking out. The Kingdom of Pontus saw the opportunity to expand its territories, as the kingdoms in Anatolia lacked Rome's protection. Mithridates VI of Pontus' first strike was against the Kingdom of Bithynia, which he conquered. He had help from some of the Greek cities in Anatolia who were rebelling against Rome. A Greek philosopher, Metrodorus of Scepsis, who was known for his hatred of Romans, advised Mithridates that he should slaughter all the Roman civilians inhabiting the region, including women and children. This action, he assured the king, would destroy Rome's grasp on the lands permanently. The date of the massacre is not known exactly, but it is presumed it happened around May of 88 BCE. Some Roman historians claim 88,000 people were killed while other sources go even higher in numbers.

This massacre provoked Rome to such an extent that they immediately proclaimed war on Mithridates and his Greek allies. The relations between the Greeks and the Romans were never the same after these events, and the Greek cities lost their Roman protection. The Roman consul Lucius Cornelius Sulla besieged Athens, who had sided with Mithridates. Sulla's armies stormed the city and took its harbor Piraeus, completely destroying it.

Sulla and Mithridates clashed with their armies at two prominent battles: the Battle of Chaeronea (86) and the Battle of Orchomenus (85). In both battles, Rome was victorious, and Sulla forced Mithridates to sign a peace treaty. The Treaty of Dardanos, signed in 85, returned everything as it was before the war. This means that Mithridates had to return the provinces of Bithynia, Cappadocia, and Paphlagonia to Rome and pay a war indemnity from his own wealth. The treaty was signed in haste since Sulla had to go back to Rome and deal with a rebellion.

Mithridates also had to deal with a rebellion in his own kingdom. He prepared a large army to deal with the uprising in Colchis, an area in today's Georgia. However, the Roman general Lucius Licinius Murena, who had stayed in Asia Minor with his garrison, saw the Pontic army's preparations as a threat to the Roman citizens of Cappadocia. He did not trust Mithridates and attacked his kingdom under the excuse of preventing another massacre of Romans, thus starting the Second Mithridatic War, which lasted from 83 to 81. Eventually, Murena invaded the territories of the Kingdom of Pontus, and Mithridates believed he was doing it under the command of Rome. Mithridates responded by attacking Roman villages and met Murena on the battlefield. The king of Pontus defeated Murena, who had to flee and seek refuge in Phrygia. Sulla did not approve of this attack on Mithridates since he did not want to break the treaty. The war ended with Mithridates making a deal with the king of Cappadocia, Ariobarzanes I. He returned some of the Cappadocian territories but kept most of what he had conquered. As a sign of peace, Mithridates engaged his own daughter, who was only four years old, to Ariobarzanes.

The Third Mithridatic war, which took place between 73 and 63, was the last and longest war between the Kingdom of Pontus and the Roman Republic. Sulla died in 78, so the strongest promoter of peace between the two nations was gone. The Roman Senate decided not to ratify the Treaty of Dardanos, as the general opinion of Rome was that Sulla was too generous when drafting the treaty and that Mithridates did not deserve to keep all the territories of his kingdom. This angered Mithridates, and he decided not to wait for the Romans to come to his kingdom. He attacked Bithynia, which was just bequeathed to Rome upon the death of its last king, Nicomedes IV. Rome sent two generals to oppose Mithridates, Lucius Licinius Lucullus and Marcus Aurelius Cotta. But Mithridates defeated Cotta at the naval Battle of Chalcedon in 74, trapping him within the city walls with no other choice but to wait for Lucullus to come to his rescue. Lucullus arrived and besieged Mithridates' army, which was occupying the city of Cyzicus at the time. Famine and plague forced Mithridates to retreat to his Kingdom of Pontus, but he was chased by Lucullus and his army, and a final battle took place in Pontus near the city of Cabira. The Roman army was victorious, and Mithridates had to run for his life to Armenia.

In Armenia, Mithridates convinced his father-in-law Tigranes II to not turn him over to Rome and to instead prepare for war. The Armenians lost all the battles against Rome, but there was some unrest in the Roman ranks. Pompey the Great had risen to power and wanted to replace Lucullus as the general of the Roman army during the Third Mithridatic War. Through scheming and inciting unrest in Lucullus' armies, Pompey was sent by the Senate to take over the command.

At the Battle of Lycus in 66, Pompey had his first victory over Mithridates, but the decisive battle was in 65 at the banks of the Abas River. Here is where Pompey defeated the main allies of Mithridates, making them unable to give further support to the king of Pontus. After this final blow, Mithridates VI fled to Crimea, where he gathered a small army in yet another attempt to regain his lost kingdom. Even his son, Pharnaces II, the king of Cimmerian Bosporus, refused to help him as Rome had just recognized his kingdom. Mithridates decided to kill his son and take the throne for himself. However, his younger son, enraged by his father's actions, raised the populace and led a rebellion. Mithridates could not bear the defeat and his own son's betrayal, so he decided to commit suicide. His death in 63 BCE marks the end of the war, and with it, the Kingdom of Pontus fell into Roman hands.

Conclusion

Even with the rising power of Rome, Anatolia managed to keep its diversity in culture and enter the new age as rich as ever. It enjoyed relative peace from the time of Rome to Constantine the Great.

Anatolia grew and developed its regions, especially after the taxes to Rome were lifted under the reign of Emperor Augustus. Agriculture boomed, as smart investments were made, and there was no lack of money. Rome also built roads throughout Anatolia, which helped the development of trade with other parts of the world. Trade enriched the already diverse culture of Anatolia by bringing merchants from exotic places such as China and various parts of Europe. It survived even the fall of the Roman Empire and set itself as a center of the civilized world through the achievements of Constantine I and the Byzantine Empire.

This is where history marks the end of the ancient times of Anatolia, a region with a rich culture that influenced the entire known world. From the Early Bronze Age to the heights of the Iron Age, Anatolia enjoyed a diversity of languages, religions, and ethnicities, even if it was constantly being torn apart by wars as countless armies marched across Anatolia. Populations moved, either migrating in the search for more fertile lands or by being relocated by ruthless kings, they all contributed to the living, breathing land that is Anatolia.

History is rich in this region, as is best shown by the constant archeological excavations that are taking place. Even today, there are many undiscovered places, whole cities that historians are still searching for. Some were probably destroyed by wars and may never be found, but there is an enormous cultural heritage in Anatolia, one is that too huge for just one book to cover.

Check out more books by Captivating History

HITTITES

A CAPTIVATING GUIDE TO THE ANCIENT ANATOLIAN PEOPLE WHO ESTABLISHED THE HITTITE EMPIRE IN ANCIENT MESOPOTAMIA

CAPTIVATING HISTORY

THE PERSIAN EMPIRE

A CAPTIVATING GUIDE TO THE HISTORY OF PERSIA, STARTING FROM THE ANCIENT ACHAEMENID, PARTHIAN, AND SASSANIAN EMPIRES TO THE SAFAVID, AFSHARID, AND QAJAR DYNASTIES

CAPTIVATING HISTORY

References

Briant, P. (2006). *From Cyrus to Alexander: a history of the Persian Empire*. Winona Lake, IN: Eisenbrauns.

Bury, J. B., Cook, S. A., & Adcock, F. (1976). *The Assyrian Empire*. Cambridge: Cambridge University Press.

Kuhrt, A. (2010). *The Persian Empire:* London: Routledge.

Matthews, R. (1998). *Ancient Anatolia*. Ankara: The British Institute of Archaeology.

Petrie, W. M. F. (1940). *Hutchinsons story of the nations: containing the Egyptians, the Chinese, India, the Babylonian nation, the Hittites, the Assyrians, the Phoenicians and the Carthaginians, the Phrygians, the Lydians, and other Nations of Asia Minor*. London: Hutchinson & Co.

River, C. (2015). *The Assyrians: the history of the most prominent empire of the ancient near east*. San Bernardino, CA.

Savage, R. (2019). *Mesopotamia: a captivating guide to ancient Mesopotamian history and civilizations, including the Sumerians and Sumerian mythology, Gilgamesh, Ur, Assyrians, Babylon, Hammurabi and the Persian Empire*.

Steadman, S. R., & McMahon, G. (2016). *The Oxford handbook of ancient Anatolia: 10,000-323 B.C.E.* Oxford: Oxford University Press.